THE COLE LECTURES FOR 1931

Delivered before

TH

THE
PRESENT-DAY SUMMONS
TO THE
WORLD MISSION OF
CHRISTIANITY

By
JOHN R. MOTT

COKESBURY PRESS
NASHVILLE

THE PRESENT-DAY SUMMONS TO THE WORLD
MISSION OF CHRISTIANITY. COPYRIGHT,
MCMXXXI, BY LAMAR & WHITMORE

TO MY WIFE

THROUGH WHOSE COMRADESHIP AS
A FELLOW TRAVELER ACROSS THE
YEARS AND ACROSS THE WORLD GOD
HAS COMMUNICATED THE MOST CRE-
ATIVE, SELF-GIVING, AND ENDURING
IMPULSES OF MY LIFE

CONTENTS

5

PREFACE

AFTER THE WORLD MISSIONARY
Conference at Edinburgh, in 1910, I was asked to prepare a book which would describe the situation then confronting the missionary forces of Christendom. This I did under the title, *The Decisive Hour of Christian Missions*. Several months ago leaders on both sides of the Atlantic expressed the desire that I render a similar service at the present time in the light of the developments of the two decades since Edinburgh, especially as they found expression in the findings and outlook of the recent world conference at Jerusalem. This request synchronized with an invitation to give the lectures on the Cole Foundation of the School of Religion of Vanderbilt University. In response to this invitation it was my privilege last April to deliver at Vanderbilt a course of six lectures on "The Present-Day Summons to the World Mission of Christianity." In transcribing them for publication I have expanded the six lectures into seven, and added three new chapters—those dealing with Race, the Indigenous Church, and the Home Base. I wish to

thank the Editor of *The International Review of Missions* for permission to incorporate into the chapter on the Home Base the larger part of the material of my recent article on "Strengthening the Home Base." A somewhat extended bibliography has been provided for the guidance of those who wish to pursue further different aspects of the subject.

It is my hope that this book may in some measure do for the Christian world at this momentous hour what I sought to accomplish in my interpretation of the world call twenty years ago.

NEW YORK, June 15, 1931   JOHN R. MOTT

THE PRESENT-DAY SUMMONS

I. WORLD TRENDS

IT WAS MY OPPORTUNITY AND privilege at the time of the World Missionary Conference at Edinburgh in 1910, and of the meeting of the International Missionary Council at Jerusalem in 1928, and during the years immediately preceding and following these gatherings, to have a somewhat exceptional exposure to the situation confronting the world mission of Christianity: first, through attendance upon both these creative assemblies, and intimate relation to their preparatory studies and their programs of conservation; secondly, through world journeys following each of these occasions and embracing areas in which are to be found over three-quarters of the inhabitants of the non-Christian world; and, thirdly, through official relationship to three organizations necessitating close touch with responsible Christian leaders of the entire world field. There is a certain advantage in moving over the world at intervals. It enables one to observe and to estimate the position, trends, and outlook of a movement of such world-wide interest and concern.

With this experience as background, it is my conviction that the past twenty years have witnessed incomparably greater changes in the world than any other period of like extent. The same is true of the world mission of Christianity itself whether one has in view its field of concern, its complexity, its pace, or its governing motives or objectives. These changes and present-day trends, if we but grasp their implications, present an irresistible summons to the Christian forces of both Occident and Orient.

It is evident that the period on which we have entered is to be the most exacting in its demands because of the forces which oppose us, the many grave and emergent issues which demand attention, and, above all, the fact that there are so many more Christians now living than ever before who have awakened to the heroic implications of the Christian Gospel. It is startling to reflect on the imminent possibility that, if we turn a deaf ear to the summons of the present most critical and fateful hour, the world mission of the Christian faith may fail. Let us fix attention on some of the more significant world trends and then pass on to heed the summons which so unmistakably comes to the Christians of the present day.

1. The spirit of nationalism is to-day manifesting greater aggressiveness and more sense of direction than ever before in the history of mankind. This is true the world over. Turkey is a good illustration. There both rulers and followers have set for themselves clearly

defined goals, and in the face of opposition of powers of the world have within a short period made startling progress toward the realization of their purposes. Their spirit and example have been contagious. Of this fact there have been many and striking evidences in Syria, Palestine, Iraq, and Arabia, and even in Egypt, India, Persia, and Afghanistan.

We are vividly conscious of the same spirit away across on the other side of Asia. Japan still impresses one as being the most national nation on the map in the sense that there one finds the spirit of patriotism burning with greater intensity, unity, and constancy than in any other land. Korea is under the Japanese rule and flag, but also under the ashes of discouragement and despair. Beneath those ashes there are bright embers that at times burst into flame. In other words, there is still such a thing as a national spirit there, just as there is in the Philippines, in India, and in parts of the Dutch Indies. On the last of my eight visits to China I was distinctly conscious for the first time of a widespread national spirit. On earlier visits I had found the spirit of nationalism in certain places or among certain limited groups. But on this recent occasion in the south, north, and east, as well as in the heart of the country, I was constantly aware of such a manifestation. This is often confusing to people in other parts of the world, because having read so much of the civil wars in China they infer that the inhabitants of different areas of the country are arrayed against each other, and that there are deep chasms of fundamental misunderstanding between them. Such, however, is not the case. These oft-recurring civil wars spring from the rival personal ambitions of certain military governors, with their paid emissaries, and, more often, their discontented unpaid emissaries. These reactionary elements, with their eyes on the past and its corrupt practices, are becoming increasingly a spent force and must inevitably give way to the more strengthening, unifying, genuinely national spirit. The chambers of commerce in China are not antagonistic to one another. The teachers' associations in different parts of the country are not out of accord. The Chinese students, who constitute an unusually important element, are not at cross-purposes. One cannot truthfully say that the people of any one section entertain bitter feelings concerning those of another section. There may be differences on minor points, but on the great guiding principles, such as those enunciated by Sun Yat-sen, there is marvelous accord. The party could not stand which did not have as a main plank in its platform that China is to be the ruler in her own house.

If possible, the developments in India of the past decade have been even more remarkable. Notwithstanding the age-long divisions between religious communities, especially the Hindu and Mohammedan, and the incomparably rigid caste compartments, the discerning visitor to India to-day, in contrast with visitors three

decades, or even one decade ago, must be profoundly impressed by the signs of a growing sense of community
of interest and common destiny. It is true that there are
still scores of millions of Indians, spread over the areas
administered by Britain and the Indian States as well,
who do not know what the word nationality means, and
who still less are conscious of possessing a national
spirit; but on the higher levels of Indian life, notably
among the intelligentsia, there are unmistakable evidences of a developing feeling of solidarity and of deepening purpose to realize certain goals. The Round
Table Conference in London was in itself an impressive
demonstration of this fact. Of course there are difficult days ahead. The British nation, in fact the British Empire, will during the years right before us have
the greatest strain put upon the patience, the self-control,
and the sense of mission to which any country in its relations to a subject people has ever been subjected.
And the Indian leaders likewise are entering upon a
period which will make unexampled demands on their
powers. In a conversation with Mahatma Gandhi at
Ahmedabad I asked him, "Which do you prefer, dominion status or complete independence?" He replied, "If
dominion status means even a little bit less than complete independence, I stand for complete independence."
Then I said: "What do you mean by independence? Do
you mean what Canada has?" To that he replied,
"Nothing could express better just what I want." I

reminded him that Canada had arrived at her present position of statehood, well characterized as full dominion status, through generations of political experience in sitting at the feet of the "mother of parliaments," and in countless practice games in local, county, provincial, and national government.

Never was the national spirit of the Latin American countries more self-conscious and vigorous. In the newly constituted and the reconstituted countries of Europe, as well as in some of the oldest, the spirit of nationalism is very marked and purposeful. Throughout the African continent one is to-day conscious of the thrill of a new life manifested in new aspirations, hopes, and ambitions.

This rising tide of nationalism and racial patriotism is a matter of profound concern to the world mission of the Christian religion. Most of the churches, especially those which constitute the Protestant communion, and increasingly the Roman Catholic communion, are committed to the policy of devolution. By this is meant that the missionaries, and the churches which sent them, hand over increasingly to the indigenous churches the power of initiative, decision, and control. This vital process is at various stages in different fields and in the work of different Christian bodies. It is a process attended with difficulty. It is never realized by a practice of drifting, procrastination, or indecision, but always by a policy of fixing definite goals, and then by resolute and, if need be, sacrificial efforts transferring a steadily increasing measure of responsibility. The time has come all over the world for great acts of trust, even if they involve, as they most certainly do, the taking of risks. It is the same with churches and nations as it is with children. The only way to insure their full development and power is to trust them with responsibility and independence. They rise to such trust. President Wilson once remarked to me that "the most conservative people in the world are students." When I expressed some doubt, he amplified his meaning by adding the words, "with heavy burdens of responsibility entrusted to them." I came to see that he was right. In my long experience with youth and in helping to plant and develop Christian organizations and movements in all parts of the world and among various races I have never regretted trusting them with great weights of responsibility.

2. Internationally, world-wide trends and outlook compare favorably with those I have found at any time since the beginning of my first-hand observation in 1895. I do not overlook certain adverse facts which would seem to contradict this contention. For example, we cannot ignore the existence and gravity of the misunderstandings among nations. It would be difficult to name a country which, judged by words and actions, understands its neighbors near and far. This is serious because misunderstandings between nations multiply

friction points, prevent fruitful coöperation, lead to collisions. Another unfavorable aspect of the international life of the world is the recent marked lowering of the prestige of Western nations in the thought and feeling of Asiatic, African, and Latin American peoples. It is not necessary at this point to enter into the causes of this unfortunate circumstance; the fact remains that they think less highly of us than they did. It should be added that there are nations, East and West, which are keenly dissatisfied with treaties and other external arrangements to which they have been committed with or without their full consent. Almost daily we are reminded that China is discontented with reference to what are well called unequal treaties, and who shall say that she has not abundant reason for her discontent? Japan is still smarting with the sense of indignity and injustice she has suffered at the hands of the American Congress. Few, if any, countries are satisfied with the Versailles Treaty. A prominent ambassador in London not long since, in speaking to me of a certain country, said of that nation, "She is oscillating between fear and cupidity." That phrase expresses aptly the varying dominating emotions of more than one nation. President Hoover, in a recent address, reminded his hearers that there were 25,000,000 men in the armies, navies, and reserves of the world, or, he added, 5,000,-000 more than there were at the beginning of the year 1914. Why, one may ask, is it found necessary to have

5,000,000 more men in armies, navies, and reserves now than it was early in 1914 unless it be that many countries are oscillating between fear and cupidity?

If adverse facts like these can be given, the question may well be raised, How can the position be maintained that on the whole the international outlook now is more reassuring than it was, for example, two and three decades ago? I would venture to support the statement by a few facts. In the first place, there are to-day twenty voices and pens speaking and writing to foster right understanding between nations and to promote good will and coöperation among them where there was one such voice or pen thus engaged twenty or thirty years ago. This is in itself a most potential fact. It means that through the influence of men who do much to affect thought and action, the attitudes and practices of peoples which might formerly have been characterized as passive or as drifting can now be spoken of as attitudes and practices of taking initiative and accepting responsibility for bringing about larger understanding and coöperation. The light is now being turned upon situations, practices, and problems which might otherwise have been the occasion of serious misunderstanding, bitterness, and strife. A good illustration is the work and influence of the Institute of Pacific Relations, which held its third session a year ago at Kyoto and its earlier sessions at Honolulu, and which is to meet next in China. This non-political body brings together every two years lead-

ing minds from all the countries around the Pacific
Basin and from other countries which have special interests in the Pacific for unhurried, thorough consideration
of the most critical problems of the Pacific areas, especially those of international concern. With judicial detachment, scientific method, and unselfish motive some of
the most inflamed situations and explosive issues have
been and are being studied, and foundations are being
laid for enduring understanding and helpful coöperation. The Williamstown Institute of Politics is exercising
a like profound and far-reaching influence. Forty years
ago there were of all the universities of the world fewer
than a score which had chairs on international relations;
now there is such provision in upwards of 150 universities and university colleges. The number of exchange
professorships between countries has also greatly multiplied. In addition to the Rhodes Trust for maintaining fellowships or scholarships in foreign countries
there are at least twelve other foundations which have
similar purposes. The League of Nations and the International Labor Office literally mark the beginning of a
new age in international understanding and coöperation. There are hundreds of international societies in
contrast with scores three decades ago. Each one of
these is constantly making for united study, thinking,
planning, and action in spheres of common interest
across national boundaries. All these and many other
agencies may be regarded as having as their distinctive

function the shedding of light internationally, and not a few of them on a world-wide scale. Light is the most important of all forces—the most far-reaching, rapid, and penetrating in its action, and the most health-giving in its influence.

Another ground for optimism regarding the international outlook is the fact that all over the world there is coming forward a new generation who expect to devote themselves to ushering in a new day in respect to furthering good will and constructive coöperation among the peoples of all lands. In countries like China and Japan they are rapidly rising into the ascendant. Within two decades, probably less, a sufficient number of them will be in positions of major importance to determine the policy and practice of the nations.

The great internationalism is the world mission of Christianity. The tens of thousands of missionaries, as ambassadors, interpreters, and mediators, are doing more than any other one factor to throw out strands of understanding friendship and unselfish collaboration between the peoples of Asia, Africa, and Latin America on the one hand and those of Europe, North America, and Australasia on the other. Their efforts are powerfully seconded or supported by such auxiliary agencies of the churches as the World's Student Christian Federation, the World Alliance for Promoting International Friendship through the Churches, the International Missionary Council, the Young Men's and Young Women's Christian Associations, and the various other youth organizations and laymen's movements. The secret of the unifying power of these bodies lies in the fact that at their center is Christ, who by His Incarnation, by the inclusiveness of His Gospel and Kingdom, by His unerring guiding principles, by His breaking down the middle wall of partition, and by the continued work of His Spirit makes possible the discovery and realization of the unity of the human race.

3. Throughout the world as a whole the present is a time of widespread unemployment, business depression, and financial stringency. Though this pressure is still severe in nearly all parts of Europe, as well as in Anglo-Saxon America and Australasia, the situation is much more serious in Asia, Africa, and Latin America. The people of these lands are under impossible economic burdens.

Japan saw one-eighth of her national wealth blotted out in forty-eight hours by the great earthquake. This is as though the United States within two days should lose $50,000,000,000. Such an overwhelming blow would have shaken any nation to the very base. It is not surprising that Japan to this day suffers from the shock. During the war she took over from other countries much manufacturing and other production which has since reverted largely to the original sources. Financial panic and unemployment ensued. Economic unsettlement still dominates the whole situation. Acute distress is felt in the rural districts. Dr. Kagawa, the great Christian social reformer, who has given much attention to the peasants, has stated that in rural areas he had recently visited the average annual income of a tenant farmer's family is 49 yen. When the 30 per cent which goes to the landowner has been subtracted, less than three yen, or only $1.50 a month, is left to meet the requirements of the entire family. The trouble is accentuated by the great congestion of the population, for fifteen persons, on the average, have to be supported on an area which in the United States would be occupied by one. In the industrial zones, where nearly half the population is found, the lot of the people seems to be quite as serious. Without doubt the present is an anxious time in Japan. The soil is congenial for the teachings of Marx and of his interpreters, Lenin and Bukharin.

In Korea, while one finds marked improvement in certain directions under Japanese rule, the greatly improved roads, for example, and the progress made in education, civil administration, sanitation, and afforestation, the economic conditions are far from satisfactory. Over 50 per cent of the farmers are in debt. This often means virtual serfdom where they must pay interest charges ranging from 24 to 36 per cent. They have emigrated by the tens of thousands to Manchuria, to Siberia, and to the mainland of Japan. It is a question, however, whether they have improved their lot by moving.

In China the situation economically as well as otherwise is chaotic, confused, and admittedly very critical. The long-drawn-out succession of civil wars alone affords an adequate explanation. In the few breathing spaces between these wars conditions have not improved because of the cruel and relentless banditry which has caused fear and uncertainty, and done much to discourage production. Add to this the terrible famine of recent years, the fearful cost of which in human life and material welfare cannot easily be exaggerated. A friend writes that the income of farmer families living in his vicinity, which is not in the famine region, ranges from $20 to $35 per annum. It is difficult to appreciate the bitterness of the struggle for existence in every part of this most populous land in the world. It is estimated that even in normal years fully eight per cent of the inhabitants are living below the level necessary for bare subsistence. What must the extent and depth of the human need and misery not be under present widely prevailing conditions? Under such circumstances it is tragic that the resources of the government must go so largely for military purposes and for debt services.

In a student conference years ago Bishop Thoburn, who had spent forty years in India, told us that in his opinion not fewer than 100,000,000 people in that country lie down each night hungry in body—that is, without having had sufficient food to satisfy the normal cravings for sustenance. In the light of my inquiries in India, it was evident that the same statement made to-day would not be an exaggeration. This is all the more noteworthy in view of the greatly improved means of communication and the remarkable irrigation works, as a result of the British administration, improvements which make impossible any recurrence of the terrible famines of former times. Sir Francis Younghusband, in his recent book, asserts that one-half of the population do not have enough food. Most of the villagers, who constitute nine-tenths of the population, are in debt. The total income of millions of families averages less than seventeen cents a day. Interest charges run all the way from 20 to 50 per cent or more. Economic slavery to unscrupulous money-lenders constitutes a stern reality.

Surely facts like these, and similar ones which might be given regarding other parts of Asia, as well as parts of Africa and Latin America, have implications for the world mission of Christianity. Most of the mission boards of the West stand for the policy of self-support on the part of rising indigenous churches. With an awareness of such conditions, they must, in seeking to realize this goal, exercise great wisdom and patience. The churches of Europe, North America, and Austral-asia should continue for a long period to devote large sums for the secure establishment of educational, medical, philanthropic, and other institutional branches of the Christian program. Moreover, there are deeper meanings for Christians everywhere. Has the Christian Gospel anything to say on the lightening or removal of such impossible economic conditions? Did Christ or did He not have such in mind when He said, "He anointed me to preach good tidings to the poor: He hath sent me to proclaim release to the captives, . . . to set at liberty them that are bruised, to proclaim the acceptable year of the Lord"? Were there unnumbered multitudes of overburdened, underpaid toilers and sufferers in His mind and heart when He gave the invitation, "Come unto me, all ye that labor and are heavy laden, and I will give you rest"? What had He in view for His followers in calling upon them to include in their prayer the petition, "Give us this day our daily bread"? May it not be that America, Britain, Canada, Holland, Germany, and other so-called Christian nations have complicity in much of the suffering of the millions of Asia and Africa, as a result of conditions which obtain because of the spread of Western industrialism or the manner of its conduct? Is it to be left chiefly to destructive, atheistic, militant communism to manifest solicitude for such sufferers and to proclaim a world-wide program of relief? Unless the Christian forces in the years right before us address themselves with greater comprehension and passion to answering these questions, their mission and message will be without power.

4. The most notable social trend of our day is the world-wide awakening and uprising of women. The changes which have been wrought in their social status and outlook during the past thirty years make a difference not of decades but of centuries. Still greater changes are now in progress. No one can foretell what the next two decades will witness.

The world over, education has been the key which has unlocked the door to higher life and greater opportunity for women. In its beginnings and early development the motive behind education was in the Western world as well as in the Eastern world a religious one. The earliest colleges in America were founded by those who wished to see women better prepared for Christian service.

Mary Lyon, in 1834, was seeking from women the first thousand dollars toward establishing the seminary which has now become Mount Holyoke College. In her own language: "It has sometimes seemed as if there was a fire shut up in my bones," and again, "Had I a thousand lives, I could sacrifice them all in suffering and hardship for its sake." What were her motives? Over and over again she says that the education here to be given was for service. "It is designed to cultivate the missionary spirit among its pupils," and she at once defines the word "missionary" as meaning that "they should live for God and do something."

On the twenty-sixth of February, 1861, Matthew Vassar, founder of the college which bears his name, read to his first board of trustees a statement of his views and wishes, from which the following extracts are taken:

"It occurred to me, that woman, having received from her Creator the same intellectual constitution as man, has the same right as man to intellectual culture and development.

"I considered that the mothers of a country mold the character of its citizens, determine its institutions, and shape its destiny.

"Next to the influence of the mother, is that of the female teacher, who is employed to train young children at a period when impressions are most vivid and lasting.

"It also seemed to me, that if woman were properly educated, some new avenues to useful and honorable employment, in entire harmony with the gentleness and modesty of her sex, might be opened to her. . . .

"To be somewhat more specific in the statement of my views as to the character and aims of the College:

"I wish that the course of study should embrace at least the following particulars: [Mr. Vassar then enumerates a number of studies] . . . last, and most important of all, the daily, systematic reading and study of the Holy Scriptures, as the only and all-sufficient rule of Christian faith and practice."

The only son of Henry Fowle Durant, the founder of Wellesley College, died when he was but a little boy. This produced a change in the father's life like that in the life of Saul of Tarsus. One day he came in from his beautiful estate and said to his wife: "How would you like to consecrate this place, which was to have been Harry's, to some special work for God?" In the words of his biographer: "With their firm and tried belief in the value and necessity of prayer, they brought their plans to God in their own simple and practical way. The Wellesley estate was reverently and whole-heartedly given to God. Whatever the future development of the work there, this much was clear: it was to aid the world in a vital and growing Christianity; something apart from creeds and dogmas; a real, living oneness with Creative Life which must of necessity shape results into higher and nobler forms than at present they could see. It had become evident to both husband and wife that woman, the mother and teacher of the race, was not equal to her task."

This man devoted all the land and all the money he had, first to God, then to the public good; and he was under fifty years of age.

In a sermon delivered from the chapel platform one Sunday morning during the first college year (1875), Mr. Durant said: "The Higher Education of Women is one of the great world battle-cries for freedom; for right against might. . . . You mistake altogether the significance of the movement of which you are a part, if you think this is simply the question of a college education for girls. I believe that God's hand is in it; that it is one of the great ocean currents of Christian civilization; that He is calling to womanhood to come up higher, to prepare herself for great conflicts, for vast reforms in social life, for noblest usefulness. The higher education is but putting on God's armor for the contest.

"We have no time now to discuss woman's mission. One fact only, as we leave it: there are three hundred thousand women teachers in the United States. Who is to govern the country? Give me the teachers!"

" 'I would rather,' he once cried passionately, 'see Wellesley College in ashes than that God should not be first in everything!' "

The most significant fact is that women everywhere owe their present enlarged opportunities to only one of the founders of the great religious systems. This is naturally more evident in those lands where other religious systems still hold sway, where life is not so complex, and, therefore, where the lives of women as affected by these systems are as yet an open book.

Generally speaking and with minor exceptions, conditions previous to the entrance of Christianity may be thus summarized: Little girls were not welcome when born, or, at best, not so welcome as boys. Education was denied them on the ground that they were incapable of learning. Marriage was absolutely the only vocation. Betrothal was arranged by parents through the agency of a middleman and was irrevocable. Child marriage was the rule. When married, a girl belonged body and soul to her husband's family. Polygamy was sanctioned and concubinage unchallenged. Divorce by the husband was possible at any time if he considered his wife jealous or too talkative, if she had no son, and for many other reasons or excuses. She could not divorce him for any cause. I have seen on the banks of the Ganges many monuments to mark the spots where in former times living widows had been burned with the dead bodies of their husbands. Widow marriage was unknown. In China mourning for life and committing suicide to show loyalty to her dead master brought honor to the widow and possibly an arch erected to her memory. To this black list of wrongs must be added words of such terrible import as infanticide—always of girls, —premature motherhood, slave girls, and "slaves of the gods" or temple girls. The amount of physical and mental suffering inherent in such conditions is beyond the imagination of those who have not seen it with their own eyes. What conception of the future life is offered by the non-Christian systems?—for women can endure much, granted only hope. What is Hinduism's offer? Be born a man. What does Mohammed offer? A paradise for men linked with the eternal degradation of women. It is a Chinese woman who says: "The Confucian message is not enough for China because it touches only half the nation." Under the sway of the ideals of these three non-Christian systems — not to mention others—live hundreds of millions of women.

One of Japan's modern women, Madame Hirooka,

owner of coal mines, bank director, and manager of her
husband's business after his death, was asked why she
had become a Christian. "I wanted women to be good,
and I wanted to help them to improve their lot. I found
I could not accomplish what I desired without religion.
That conclusion sent me to study religion from the
woman's point of view. I found that there is no hope
for women in any of the religions of the Orient. They
teach that from the cradle to the grave women are in-
ferior to men. . . . When I read the Gospels of Jesus I
found that Jesus made no distinction between the sexes.
I liked that. We are all, women as well as men, children
of God. I came to the conclusion that the only way for
the women of the Orient to attain their true position is
through Christianity." [1] Madame Hirooka has spoken
the universal word, for the Gospel alone has brought
the message that woman also has a personal responsibility to the Living God, and here lies the root of all
freedom.

How schools for little girls were first started by missionary women in various lands is a fascinating story.
Education — even a little — brought self-respect, then
in the course of years the possibility of economic independence, and thus all other gifts in its train. Very
gradually ever since those early schools, many of which
have grown into high schools and colleges, were estab-

[1] Madame Hirooka, in *The Place of Women in the Church on the
Mission Field*, pp. 15 f. (New York: The International Missionary Council, 1927). Used by permission.

lished, the age of marriage has been rising and some freedom of choice is being given, veils are lifting, purdahs are opening, minds are awakening, hope is coming. Isabella Thoburn College in Lucknow and Women's Christian College, Madras, India; American Mission College, Cairo; Constantinople Woman's College; Ginling and Yenching in China; Lovedale and Amanzimtoti Institutes in South Africa; Woman's Christian College of Japan and Kobe College; and many others are the eloquent and irrefutable testimony to the work of Christian missionaries through long, patient years.

The general trend has been upward and outward and onward, and since the Great War the acceleration is ever more rapid. T. Z. Koo says: "The women of China are no longer confined to the domestic sphere. They are coming out in a remarkable manner into public life. In education, business, government, medicine, and so forth, Chinese women are rapidly taking their places. The barrier in the social intercourse between the sexes is also coming down. Young men and young women are to-day meeting freely in society. As an indication of the new status already acquired by our women, we need only look at the membership of the Central Administrative Council, the highest organ in our national government. The Council is composed of fifteen members, and the chairman of the group is, *ex officio*, President of the Republic. At one time, this council of fifteen had two women members on it. The women of China, therefore, need no longer fight for the vote, or for equality before the law, or for the privilege to enter the professions. All these opportunities are already open to them. The only limit to the full use of these opportunities lies in the fact that we have not been able to provide enough facilities for the education and training of our women." [2]

The women of Japan are in their possibilities second to none. They are seeking legal, social, political, and educational equality with their men folk. Wisely they are putting chief emphasis on education so as to be prepared.

It is estimated that 99 per cent of the boys and girls of Japan are in the elementary schools—a showing hardly surpassed in the world. When high-school age is reached, most girls must stop. There are not schools enough. Rigid examinations are the test of fitness, and there are several well-qualified applicants for every one who can be admitted. The same is true of the colleges. This hunger for education is one of the striking phenomena of present-day Japan.

Formerly no women, with the exception of courtesans, were engaged in work outside their homes. Now there are many millions. Statistics show more than 1,250,000 in factories; 50,000 in mines; 1,100,000 in professional work, such as medical, educational, com-

[2] T. Z. Koo, in *The Annals of the American Academy of Political Science*, Vol. 152, November, 1930, p. 13.

mercial; and some 6,000,000 in agriculture. They are attempting anything and almost everything. They are doctors, nurses, teachers, clerks, journalists, philanthropists. Stenography, typewriting, and the telephone are largely in their hands. They are in banks, post offices, and railway stations. The law was the last profession to open for women, but three imperial universities now admit women as regular students in law.

This process of industrialization and the consequent partial or total economic independence are making great changes in the social structure of Japan. The contact with the outside world and with men is tending to break down the family system—for millenniums the bulwark of the civilization of Japan and of the whole Orient.

Women are agitating for various reforms. Madame Yajima was for a generation the great temperance leader. They are making strenuous efforts to abolish the notorious Yoshiwara. The President of the Supreme Court in 1927 recognized for the first time the right of a married woman to take legal proceedings against her husband for misconduct and to sue for divorce. About five years ago a questionnaire was sent to a large number of the most modern women asking what reforms were most urgently needed. They wanted a great many, but the six which had the largest number of votes were:

(1) Society should know the real condition of the working woman; (2) the architecture of the Japanese house ought to be changed so that a servantless life could

be lived; (3) women should have the same educational advantages, the same legal rights, and the same pay for the same work as men; (4) the reformation of customs, especially those that are largely formal and have no positive value, is needed; (5) the removal from the men's minds of the idea that men are lords, and women slaves, is urgently necessary; (6) women need freedom.

In 1930 a bill proposing the grant of voting rights to women in the municipal and rural bodies passed the Lower House with the support of members of the Government Party. The bill was vetoed by the House of Peers. The Associated Press carried a telegram dated Tokyo, March 24, 1931: "The House of Peers, for the second time, blocked to-day a proposal granting equal franchise rights to women. A bill which passed the House of Representatives a month ago was snowed under in the upper session."

Nowhere have the changes been more revolutionary or come more quickly for a whole people than in Moslem Turkey. The slogan of old Turkey was "Slowly, slowly"; but now it would be more truly expressed by "Faster, faster." The Turkish women have always been in the front line of progress among the Moslem women of the world. The women's movement has differed from that in other lands in that it has been more truly a part of the national transformation.

In the few years since the Great War all of life is changed for all the people. Instead of the Koran as the basis of all law, civil as well as religious, the Turkish Republic has taken its penal code from the Italian, its civil from the Swiss, and its commercial from the German laws. Polygamy is now, of course, forbidden. The end of the war also brought the end of seclusion and the veil.

Education is based on the absolute equality of men and women. President Mustapha Kemal encourages professional education for women, and medicine and law are the most popular subjects. Many women are now in the medical department of the Turkish University. The government helped the first two women graduates in law to secure positions.

There are women's magazines, literary and philanthropic clubs, and excellent women speakers. Halidé Edib, now well known as author and lecturer, has been a pioneer in many lines. She was the first Turkish woman to receive the degree of bachelor of arts; to electrify Turkey by her speeches during the war; to help in organizing the new republic; to take a prominent part in the Institute of Politics at Williamstown, Massachusetts, in 1928. Recently she delivered a course of lectures at Barnard College on Turkish history.

Turkish women now vote on educational matters, and have the right to stand as candidates and to vote at municipal elections and elections for the Grand National Assembly. Two women have been appointed judges, in Angora and Constantinople.

The Simon Commission in relation to India reported: "In seven provinces out of nine, women may now be members of the legislatures . . . and members of the Legislative Assembly. . . . The vanguard of progressive women is . . . fired with an intense desire to enlist the womanhood of the country for more effective national service."

The All-India Women's Conference on Educational and Social Reform is a very significant factor in creating sentiment to back up social reforms. They plead for freedom, an equal status, and an equal education with men. What is being accomplished is shown by the passing of the Sarda Bill making illegal and punishable the marriage of girls under fourteen years of age; and by the act passed in Madras, under the leadership of Mrs. Reddi, vice-president of the Madras Legislative Council, setting free the slave girls of the temples to follow any calling they please. They are seeking the revision of inheritance laws and the abolition of polygamy and purdah. This conference states its high ideals as follows: "Moral training, based on spiritual ideals, should be compulsory for all schools and colleges, and the spirit of social service should be inculcated." That the women of India must be taken into account is proved by the way Mahatma Gandhi has sought their help, and by the fact that he appointed Mrs. Naidu to take his place as leader of the Swaraj while he was in prison. Quite as remarkable—an Indian woman sitting as a regular delegate at the Round Table Conference in London.

Miss Alice B. Van Doren, long of India, well sums up this trend: "Throughout India, as through nearly every country of the Orient, has swept during the last decade a swift and irresistible urge, snatching women from the ways of age-long custom and setting their feet upon paths of new adventure. This 'Women's Movement' has given to educated women a new freedom of thought and an entrance into professional and political life and social service. The educated Indian woman, from being a mere unit in the family or caste, has suddenly entered upon the estate of an individual, with powers of self-choice and self-determination, with all the opportunities and all the dangers of individualistic life opening before her."

Every period of transition has its dangers, but the present is heavy-laden with them. When old religions and social sanctions are going or gone and no others equally binding are being substituted, there must be confusion and human wreckage. Almost too quickly are these women breaking out from seclusion and oppression and restraints into the swift currents of this modern age. In early days, girls were sheltered as well as educated in Christian schools only; now the majority are in government secular schools.

[3] Alice B. Van Doren, in *The Christian Task in India* (John McKenzie, Editor), p. 43 (London: Macmillan & Co., 1929).

They also study abroad. Just now the number in the United States from Japan, China, the Philippines, Korea, India, and Turkey is 550. No one can estimate the influence of each one of these as she returns to her native land. We might make the attempt by thinking of each one as one thousand. Mrs. Herman Liu comments in a suggestive way on the results of study abroad: "It is very interesting to notice that returned girl students . . . from America usually become doctors, social workers. A great many of them marry and become better home-makers. Returned girl students from England are practically all teachers and usually stay single; from France they are usually 'free in their thinking'; while from Russia they are revolutionists, and, nay, Communists, too!"

If we count all who are in any way prepared to lead through the present confusion, not only Christians but all in the vanguard of reform, their numbers are pitifully small compared with the vast host behind them: approximately 150,000,000 in India, 180,000,000 in China, 40,000,000 in Japan and Korea, 100,000,000 in Moslem lands. What a work awaits the little bands who will inevitably give direction to the multitude! This is the time for all of us, if ever, to become partners with opportunity and adventurers for God. "Rise up, ye women that are at ease, and hear my voice; ye careless daughters, give ear unto my speech. . . . Tremble, ye women that are at ease; be troubled, ye careless ones. . . .

Blessed are ye that sow beside all waters. . . . Now therefore hear this, thou that art given to pleasures, that
sittest securely."

In the words of Mary Lyon: "This object . . . penetrates
too far into futurity and takes in too broad a view to
discover its claims to the passing multitude. We appeal
in its behalf to wise men who can judge what we
say. We appeal to those who can venture as pioneers
in the great work of renovating a world. Others may
stand waiting for the great multitude to go forward." [4]

5. In the realm of education we witness developments, emphases, and tendencies of great significance.
Within the past two or three decades there has been
throughout Asia and in parts of Africa and the Pacific
island world a great multiplication of universities, colleges, and schools under government or other secular
control. In these areas, as in the West, the increase in
enrollment of students has been enormous. Whereas
formerly the attendance upon these institutions was
drawn largely from more favored groups, it is becoming increasingly democratic.

More and more the emphasis is being laid upon the
purely secular or materialistic. This is seen in the cur-
ricula, in the expenditure on equipment, and in the
general influence on the studying youth.

The World War has exerted a profound influence on

[4] Beth Bradford Gilchrist, *The Life of Mary Lyon*, p. 233 (New York:
Houghton Mifflin Company, 1910).

government educational policy. Much of the emphasis
on applied science, and on making the centers of learning more largely tributary to exploiting natural resources and to augmenting the intellectual power of the
country, is traceable to this cause. During the war
propaganda was reduced to a science, and, in the light
of the experiences of those fateful days, governments
have become more jealous and vigilant with reference
to the factors which make and control opinion, feeling,
and attitudes. Chief among these factors is education.
The war also gave an unprecedented impetus to the spirit
of intense nationalism and the will to self-determination. Governments have fostered this spirit in their
educational systems. In virtually every land the students have been in the forefront in the outbursts of nationalism.

Thus we find advancing by leaps and bounds vast
secular systems of education with limitless governmen-
tal resources and authority at their back. At the best
their attitude toward religion is neutral. In practical
effect, however, it is more often antireligious. The net
influence all over the non-Christian world is to develop
indifference toward all religion. This tendency is
strengthened by the aggressive propaganda of antireligious movements, such as the New Thought Movement of a decade ago in China, the present Dangerous
Thoughts Movement in Japan, and everywhere the in-

sidious cell activity as well as indirect influence of the Russian Communistic Youth Movement.

The result is that the traditional beliefs of vast numbers of students in the lands of the non-Christian religions have been undermined; and in many nominally Christian countries, such as those of Latin America, Southeastern and Eastern Europe, and Western Asia, the students have become, as the Germans say, *konfessionslos*—that is, without religious affiliation. One cannot without alarm contemplate this trend. What could be more serious than a leadership for the generation of to-morrow without the anchoring, guiding, and uplifting power of reasonable and vital religious faith?

Happily, by the side of many of these non-Christian systems of education, the world mission of Christianity has established its own educational work. In many a field it has been the actual pioneer of modern learning. The value of the contribution it has thus made in the Far East, in the Near East, in Southern Asia, in the Nile Valley, and in wide areas of Bantu Africa could hardly be overstated. Its work is by no means accomplished. In view of educational trends such as those at which we have glanced, is it not evident that its greatest contribution will be called for in the next two decades?

If the cause of Christian education is to triumph in the face of this grave situation, it must concentrate on the qualitative, as contrasted with the quantitative, aspect of its program. It cannot hope in the matter of numbers to keep pace with the government and other purely secular institutions, but in the realm of character building—the development of the entire personality—it can, if it will, not only excel but also make an indispensable spiritual contribution which no government or other secular agency can supply. The supreme advantage of Christian education is that it seeks to counteract the destructive effects of the purely intellectual approach by providing education for the whole of life. To this end, while the Christian educational movement must preserve and strengthen its position of respect and influence in point of the thoroughness, up-to-dateness, and truly progressive character of its intellectual leadership and processes, it must with conviction make its major contribution in the sphere of religious education. Its chief and constant concern must be its product in character and spirit. This involves paying great prices. It must turn a deaf ear at times to alluring appeals to concern itself chiefly with large numbers. Rather let it deliberately and resolutely center on developing only so many institutions as can be maintained with the highest Christian efficiency. This principle, in turn, involves preserving at all costs an adequate staff—adequate in number and in intellectual ability and adequate in contagious Christian conviction and character. Central in all their thinking, planning, contacts, and service will be the influencing of the motives, the springs of idealism, the action of the will through laying secure thought-bases of faith and through exposure to the Ever-Living and Ever-Creative God as revealed in Jesus Christ.

Another heavy responsibility must rest upon Christians throughout the world as they contemplate the educational task, and that is to meet another dangerous trend in the educational realm—that of the serious restrictions being placed upon religious education in general. There are multiplying indications that the battle of religious liberty will have to be fought once again in the years immediately before us. To this end the leaders of the Christian forces need to arrive at a common mind and then with all wisdom, patience, and courage make that mind known.

6. It is impossible to characterize in any adequate general terms the religious trends and outlook, because the religious forces are so numerous and varied, and are manifesting such widely different aspects. The impression which one to-day receives from face-to-face contacts with the non-Christian religions is that of gradual disintegration. Under the influence of modern science, secular civilization, and historical criticism, as well as of the world mission of Christianity, these systems of faith are losing their hold as sources of vital energy and as practical regulative influences on life. This is particularly true of the educated classes. Here and there, to be sure, one finds evidences of revival,

but these are confined largely to the realm of research or study, and exhibit little energizing and transforming power in the sphere of individual life and human relations. Their concern seems to be more that of conserving the heritage of the past than that of meeting the demands of the present and of the coming day. A more hopeful sign is that presented by new cults or reform movements within some of the ancient faiths. These, however, seem to be powerless to resist or stay the widespread break-up or weakening. The most serious aspect of the situation is that in all the non-Christian lands there is coming forward a generation which has largely thrown off the restraints and directive power of the old religions and ethical systems, and is facing the exacting demands of the new day without guiding principles and the anchoring or conserving power of traditions and social sanctions which have dominated long centuries of ancestry. Recognition should be made of syncretic schools of thought and action, but at their best they constitute a lifeless mosaic of unrelated fragments and are apparently powerless to meet life's deepest spiritual demands.

At no time in modern centuries have there been such extensive and aggressive antireligious movements. One of these broke out in China about a decade ago. It was directed more especially at Christianity which, it maintained, was imperialistic, capitalistic, and unscientific. This has largely died down; but there are not wanting signs of a fresh outbreak. This is in part due to the propaganda of the Russian communistic movement, which with its announced world program, able leadership, passion, and generous financial backing cannot be ignored. It is one of the most sinister facts in the entire world.

Though one cannot speak of the prevailing secular civilization as an organized movement, it nevertheless with its associated schools of naturalistic philosophy, of behaviorist psychology, and of that phase of humanism which denies the superhuman constitutes by common consent the most serious menace to religion in all forms.

The Church of Rome is manifesting increased missionary interest and activity. There has been in recent years a marked growth in its financial income and expenditure and in the number of its missionaries, particularly in the Orient. The interest manifested by the youth the past two decades has been notable. The statesmanlike attitude of the present Pope toward the missionary program of the Church has had large influence. The Missionary Exposition held in the Vatican on his initiative has served to widen the interest.

The Eastern Orthodox communion in recent centuries has been lacking in missionary spirit and activity. The one great exception to this generalization is the remarkable work of the Russian Church of Japan, which is one of the most successful and fruitful pieces of missionary work of modern times. The severe persecutions and suffering of the Armenian, Russian, and Greek Churches within the past two decades, with the attendant wide dispersions, may ultimately result, as in other periods in the life of the Christian Church, in burning out the dross and in quickening the missionary spirit.

The Protestant communion in its missionary work labors under certain handicaps. One is that of its many divisions. While these divisions have, as a rule, had justification in the lands of their origin, their perpetuation on the mission fields under present conditions would seem to be unnecessary and unwise. Another handicap under which the Protestant, as well as the Roman Catholic, missions suffer is that of their associations. In the eyes of non-Christian peoples the work of these churches of the West is naturally associated with the countries from which the missionaries come, and all too often there proceed from these same countries influences of an evil or questionable character. Thus the innocent suffer for the guilty. Notwithstanding these and many other handicaps, including those traceable to the dislocations of the World War, Protestant missions the world over abound in encouragement. First of all, the fact that the leaders recognize clearly the shortcomings and the need of a fresh orientation to the great task is most hopeful. The measures which are being taken by mission boards, singly and collectively, to restudy their work through evaluation conferences, through objective studies by individual experts and by special commissions sent out for the purpose, are attended with large promise. The countless retreats by the workers on the various fields are releasing fresh creative energy. The associating of leading minds in different lands in the West for clarifying and defining the issues before the world mission and for intensive study of the Christian message is striking at the heart of the deepest need. The wider recognition of the social implications of the Gospel is a healthy sign. Over against the divisive tendencies within and outside the churches is the ever-growing movement in the direction of closer coöperation and unity both in the so-called home-base countries and in those to which the missionaries are sent. The most significant and potential single fact was the world missionary meeting held on the Mount of Olives in 1928 —in many respects the most creative and prophetic religious gathering of modern times.

Notwithstanding any handicaps which the world mission of Christianity may suffer because of divisions between or within the great Christian communions, the overmastering fact is that the influence of Jesus Christ was never so widespread, so penetrating, and so transforming as it is to-day. It is impossible to furnish accurate figures, but it is probably a conservative estimate, based on such returns as are available, to say that fully twenty millions of men and women in non-Christian areas of Asia and Africa are now looking to Christ for guidance, for redemption, and for power infinitely greater than

human, where there were less than two millions looking Christward thirty years ago. If this be true, it is a
stupendous fact.

Moreover, the Christward movement is gathering
momentum from decade to decade. Quite as significant
as Christ's conquest of individual lives is His ever-
widening sway over whole areas of life and of human relationships. There are multiplying signs on every continent of the quickening of the social conscience. One
might almost maintain that Jesus Christ creates the social
conscience. Be that as it may, of one thing we are certain: that where He is best known and obeyed there we
find conscience most sensitive and responsive. It re-
calls the Puritan paradox, "With increasing holiness
grows the sense of sin." It is highly significant that
more and more in the lands of the non-Christian religions Christ is being recognized as the last court of appeal
in morals. "He stands before men as plainly greater
than Western civilization, greater than the Christianity
that the world has come to know."

II. THE SUMMONS OF RURAL LIFE

Throughout the vast areas of Asia, Africa, and Latin America there is overwhelming need that Christianity in its world-wide outreach place far stronger emphasis than hitherto on serving the rural communities. It has been asserted in a recent conference that, whereas nine-tenths of the population of Asia and Africa are living in villages and the countryside, the missionary forces are devoting only one-tenth of their personnel and of their financial expenditure to work on behalf of these nine-tenths. Though this may be an exaggeration in respect to limited fields here and there, my studies have convinced me that in the main this contention is supported by the facts. The question might be raised, Have those who hold this view taken into account that many workers located in cities are engaged in service which benefits the rural communities as well as the cities? Probably this consideration has not been kept in view in every instance, but even where adequate allowance has been made the impression still remains that relatively the rural fields present the areas of greatest neglect. Personally I would not counsel devoting less attention to the claims of the cities and to the institutional work so largely centered in the cities, but would urge that the time has come, in fact is long overdue, when a much larger number of the ablest missionaries, and a marked increase in the amount of mission funds, should be assigned to the all-too-neglected rural communities. It is also important that among all who are to serve rural fields there be developed more genuine rural-mindedness. Far too many are actually working in the country without an appreciation of the special needs of country people.

The rural population of the fields with which the world mission is specially concerned numbers approximately one billion. Of this number, over 750,000,000 are in Asia. In Japan 52 per cent of the population are in the country; in Korea, 90 per cent. In China it is estimated that 85 per cent are outside the cities; in India 90 per cent live in more than 700,000 villages. Most of the 170,000,000 of Africa, with the exception of those in twenty or thirty cities, live under rural conditions.

The need of these rural areas is not only extensive but likewise intensive. In the villages even more than in the cities must be waged the conflict with ignorance, poverty, disease, and sin. With the exception of Japan and a negligibly small number of districts in certain other countries, the rate of illiteracy among the rural populations is alarmingly great, ranging from 40 to over 90 per cent.

As has been emphasized, the economic lot of the peasant or village population is desperate. In Japan two-thirds of the farmers are full or part tenants, fighting against poverty, and carrying an aggregate indebtedness in excess of $2,000,000,000. In Korea conditions are correspondingly bad. The Indian peasant, as a rule, is poor and hopelessly in debt, and is consequently underfed and an easy prey to disease. Though reliable statistics are not available for China, exploratory visits and studies made by missionaries in various parts of the country do not, except in rare instances, afford a brighter picture. Professor Ross has called attention to the fact that all the way down the west coast of Latin America, from Mexico to the southern extremity of South America, much of the agricultural labor can best be characterized as peonage.

Rural Africa is fairly reeking with disease. Some unconquered diseases of grave peril to mankind have their chief abode there. The extensive tropical areas of India, the Pacific island world, and Latin America, which will for many a day be zones of conflict against this great enemy, have scarcely been entered and are virtually unserved by the modern medical profession. So far as the village life is concerned the ministry of health education, child welfare, and sanitation is relatively unknown. The exceptions are so very few and far between as to make the general black background of physical human need and suffering overwhelmingly appalling.

How sadly true it is, also, that the haunts and strongholds of darkest and densest superstition are the villages of the non-Christian world. Here may be found animism in its crudest forms—a religion of fear and despair— and the most deadening and enslaving influences of the non-Christian faiths. Even strife among social, racial, and religious groups and castes breaks out in greatest bitterness in the midst of village life conditions. Though all these and other evils and adverse conditions exist in cities as well as in the country, they are to a far greater extent unrelieved and unopposed in the villages.

A young Christian worker struck off in a few minutes and sent me the following list which affords a concrete, vivid but not overdrawn picture of a typical Indian village before constructive Christian influences were brought to bear upon it. With variations similar side lights might be thrown on village life and conditions which obtain in other lands where rural problems have been neglected:

Every family has a well bucket. Not kept clean.
Wells not properly supervised.
Clothing washed on edge of well. Soiled water runs back into well again.
No drains for waste water.
No girls' school.
No library and no books.
Illiterate women and girls.

No occupation for boys who don't go to school.

Dead animals left about.

Pigs all over village.

Only two waste barrels and those not used.

Refuse left in middle of alleys.

Housing below sanitary standards, too few **windows, too low** doors, no ventilation, too many people per room.

Cattle in houses and badly kept cattle.

Unscreened meat sold in markets.

Flies (black with them).

Standing water and consequent mosquito pest.

No paving, and roads almost impassable in rains.

Lepers.

Unlimited pariah dogs.

Considerable tuberculosis and no segregation.

Hakkims or native doctors (and often very expensive).

Untrained midwives.

Universal giving of opium to babies.

No health instruction for mothers, prenatal or other kinds.

Superstitions interfering with safe childbirth and after care.

Every baby fed every time it cries.

Most babies put to sleep in tight cloth hammocks.

No place to leave babies when mothers go to work.

Babies entrusted to too young children while parents are at work.

Late nights for children and no rest during day. Excessive nervousness due to overfatigue.

Child labor; carrying of too heavy water jars, etc.

Every year in certain seasons whooping cough, measles, chickenpox, enteric, mumps, malaria, dysentery, pneumonia, influenza.

Many children unwashed, uncombed.

Skin and eye diseases everywhere.

Pyorrhea.

At least one-third of the children undernourished because of poverty or ignorance.

No care of sick.

No control of communicable diseases.

Unsupervised and uncontrolled cases of insanity.

Superstitions interfering with care of fevers of all kinds.

No recreations or occupation for leisure time for either sex, aside from an occasional *bhajan* (devotional song).

Part-time labor due to cotton gins and idleness part of year.

Beggars.

Hopeless indebtedness.

Gambling.

Standard of living too low in many instances for adequate food.

Habit of sitting and sleeping on damp mud floors and consequent rheumatism.

Use of *pan* (betel nut) out of proportion to income.

Not enough food for animals.

Mohammedan women in semi-purdah.

No fruit trees.

Hindu vs. Mohammedan, and inter-caste feeling.

Vital statistics casual or unreported.

Certain depressed classes eat dead animals.

Mothers-in-law in control.

Polygamy.

Prostitution.

No laws to enable us to stop cruelty to women and children.

Another list could be drawn up quite as graphic and appealing which would throw light on the terrible handicaps and burdens of rural populations of non-Christian lands often suffering from partial or acute famine due to drought, inadequate irrigation, lack of flood control and afforestation; to improper or antiquated methods of cultivation and care of the soil; to poor seed selection, marketing, transportation, and financing; to ignorance as to how to control animal and plant pests and diseases; and, in India, to the supposed sacredness of all animal life.

The rural field constitutes not only one of the greatest areas of neglect but also one which presents claims of the utmost importance upon the attention of the world mission of Christianity. These problems are not of merely academic interest but of supreme concern. On their solution the comfort, welfare, and destiny of whole peoples and nations depend. Such basic elements as the following are involved in the solution: the food supply for unnumbered millions; the raw materials needed by industries on which the wide world is dependent; to a larger degree than is often realized, the man power needed by industry; and the market for consumption of much that is being produced in the centers of population. It is well that people of the West remind themselves more often than they do of their dependence upon the toil and well-being of peasants of Asia, Africa, and the Pacific islands—for instance, for supplies of rice, tea, coffee, sugar, rubber, leather, spices, drugs, cotton, silk, dyes, oils, and also for essential elements entering into the making of steel and other manufactures. Thus we are dependent upon them for food and clothing. Not a train, or motor car, or ocean liner could be built or move without their labor. We are thus tied up directly to them by economic strands which involve moral and spiritual responsibility.

Moreover, with the rapid growth of democracy on all

continents the political importance of the rural population is of growing significance. How true it is that the country population is one of the conserving, stabilizing, anchoring factors in the life of nations. Throughout the long life of Japan the peasant has stood socially and in dignity next to the Samurai or knightly class; and in China for thousands of years next to the literati. It is interesting to observe how in our day all over the world governments are paying more and more attention to problems of rural welfare. In many countries on both sides of the Atlantic in recent years there have been important government commissions working on these problems, and much progressive legislation has resulted. Similar bodies have been at work in Africa and India, as well as in the Far East and the Near East. Gandhi has insisted that India's problems will be settled in the villages, and has made the lifting of the untouchables (who are found chiefly in villages) one of the main planks of his platform. In this connection it is suggestive that both Hindu and Mohammedan communities have, from political considerations, begun to manifest special interest in these village outcastes. The Russian communistic forces in their policies and propaganda both inside Russia and in other lands are concerning themselves very particularly with peasant populations.

The Christian Church, above all other bodies and forces, should be aflame with interest and burdened with concern for the rural populations of the entire non-Christian world. Though it has undoubtedly been in line with Providential leading or purpose that we should in all these lands have begun our work in the cities and large towns, there can be no shadow of doubt that the present world-wide agrarian awakening, as well as all the other considerations mentioned above, challenge the churches and their auxiliary agencies to address themselves as never before to this vast area of human need and neglect. This is Christianity's opportunity. The doors are open on every hand. Wherever they have been entered, and adequate forces have given themselves to the task of cultivation, the results have been highly encouraging. For example, Bishop Azariah of India points out that of the Christians in India, numbering more than 4,500,000, 93 per cent are in the villages. He significantly adds that in the rural church is found the evidence of greatest dynamic for self-support, self-propagation, and self-government.

The objectives before the Christian movement as it confronts the rural field might be summarized as follows:

1. To bring the members of the community under the influence of Christ; to develop in them symmetrical Christian character; to draw them together in Christian fellowship; and to enlist them in Christian service.

2. To help them secure healthful living conditions.

3. To see that guidance is afforded for the proper cultivation of their material resources so as to insure necessary food supply and a sound economic development of the community.

4. To advance the educational and recreational life of young and old.

5. To foster the improvement of home or family life.

6. To promote right social relations, community spirit, and coöperative effort.

This conception of rural uplift is genuinely Christian. Its sanction is found in Jesus Christ Himself, for it is implicit in His Gospel and commands. Its realization will insure the abundant life both individually and socially which He came to bring unto men. Its outworking as set forth in the following statement by Dr. Sam Higginbottom, the head of the Agricultural Institute near Allahabad, India, is in striking contrast with what obtains where the influence of Christ's principles and spirit is not brought to bear:

"How is it that one stratum of Indian life under one system makes such a poor showing in progressive living and cumulative achievement? Part of this stratum is either entirely stationary or going backwards. Part of it takes Jesus Christ as its Lord and Master, as well as its example and model, and immediately the old things pass away; and the part that follows Jesus Christ enters literally here and now a new heaven and a new earth. Children, both boys and girls, are educated. Medical care is given. Sanitation finds a place in daily life. Disease is prevented. Economic conditions are greatly im-

proved. Higher education is enjoyed by many, who take their
place in the public life of the people of India. Moral conditions improve. Wherever the Bible goes and its precepts are
followed, there the standard of all human relationships is
raised.

"It is the social and religious system, not the individual,
that makes the difference. Christ is the Life and the Power
in the system, religious, social, economic, political, and moral.
The way to develop a full belief in India would be to study
the history of the Indian Protestant Christian community.
This history would show that India is not hopeless and incapable of improvement. While it is true that many Indian
Christians came from the best blood and social traditions of
non-Christian India, yet a large majority of the Indian Protestant Christian community have come from the outcaste and
untouchable classes. Jesus Christ has exalted them. . . .

"Now, in India, Christian missions have been pioneers in
much that has stood for the betterment of the people. The
direct preaching of the gospel of love and salvation, the educational work of missions, the medical work of missions, the
literary work of missions, the social work of missions, the
industrial work of missions, the agricultural work of missions
are all done by men and women who recognize that God is
using their differing gifts to express one great, controlling
motive and purpose: that God so loved the Indian world that
He gave His only begotten Son, that whosoever believeth in
Him should not perish, but have everlasting life." [1]

One of the most encouraging developments of the
present day is the awakening of interest and recognition of responsibility on the part of Christians to accept
the challenge presented by the rural situation. A major
cause of this has been the recent Meeting of the International Missionary Council, which in its preparatory

[1] Sam Higginbottom, in *The Christian Task in India* (John Mc-
Kenzie, Editor), pp. 162 f. (London: Macmillan & Co., 1929).

activities, in its deliberations and findings, and in its subsequent propaganda has served to lift the whole subject into a place of proper prominence. The Korean Rural Survey conducted by Dr. Edmund de S. Brunner of the Institute of Social and Religious Research and presented at Jerusalem as a model of its kind; the pooling at Jerusalem of knowledge, experience, and insight of leading authorities from all parts of the world on various phases of work for rural populations; the statesmanlike policy adopted on that occasion; the series of notable visits to South Africa, to India, and to the Far Eastern countries by Dr. Kenyon L. Butterfield, one of the outstanding minds in all that pertains to the improvement of country life conditions; the collaboration of Dr. Thomas Jesse Jones, whose lifelong studies and unique experience as the head of two constructive commissions to Africa enabled him to exert a most valuable influence on the evolution of forward-looking policies; the dynamic leadership afforded by Dr. Kagawa in his work on behalf of the peasants of Japan; the large attention given to rural problems in the recent meetings of the national Christian councils of India, China, Japan, Siam, and the Congo; and the chain of conferences held along the pathway of the world journeys of the chairman and secretaries of the International Missionary Council; together with the prophetic leadership afforded by the all-too-small band of devoted agricultural missionaries and advocates, such as Dr. John H.

Reisner, Mr. F. L. Chang, and Mr. G. W. Groff of China, Dr. Sam Higginbottom, the Reverend W. H. Wiser, and Mr. K. T. Paul of India, Mr. Benjamin H. Hunnicut of Brazil, Mr. D. S. Bullock of Chile, and Mr. George A. Roberts of Rhodesia; and the excellent work of the Near East Foundation in the Levant—and all within the very recent past—have, let us believe, ushered in a new day.

In the light of all this splendid initiative and the commanding vision of the Jerusalem Meeting on the Mount of Olives, as well as in response to the stern yet inspiring challenge which comes from the areas of rural need and neglect, the following concrete proposals are put forth as a constructive program:

1. The concerted, constructive thinking and experimentation by the present leaders in rural work should be carried forward to develop an adequate, accepted apologetic for agricultural mission work which will be recognized by missionary administrators, donors, and advocates, and accorded a place coördinate in importance and provision with that given to medical or educational work. Such is far from being the case to-day. Dr. Reisner has recently stated that of approximately 18,000 missionaries representing North American boards in all parts of the world only about 100 are recorded as agricultural missionaries, and he reminds us that this represents a growth of more than twenty years. A more careful analysis reveals that probably not more

than half of this small number had received specialized
training for their work in the sense that the medical missionaries do. It must be understood that the word "agricultural" here connotes far more than the technique of
farm practice. It comprises the whole range of problems involved in the livelihood of a great majority of
the human race. Agriculture is an economic and social
problem of the first magnitude.

2. There is need of making in all extensive rural
areas throughout the world comprehensive, thorough
fact-finding surveys, similar to those conducted in Korea
by Dr. Brunner. This has become a truism in the realm
of industry, commerce, and finance. It has been recognized as necessary in educational missionary work, as
witness the surveys conducted in China, India, the Near
East, and Africa and now in prospect for Japan. Another interesting survey of a rural field is just now
under way, the one being conducted under the auspices
of the National Christian Council of Siam by Professor Zimmerman of Harvard University. It covers the
entire field of that country, which is largely rural. The
enlightened Siamese Government is coöperating in every
possible way, having allocated many officials to assist
Professor Zimmerman, and having placed the railway
and other facilities at his disposal.

3. In each field the national Christian council, representing all the Christian forces, should, in the light
of knowledge and experience already gained, or of new

surveys and expert guidance, formulate a statesman-like program. It should re-state objectives; set forth concretely the policy to be followed locally, sectionally, and nationally; deal realistically with measures involving coöperation and relationships; indicate an order of priorities as to occupation of different fields, employment of different means, and placing of different emphases; and, above all, should grapple ably with matters of finance, leadership, and training.

4. The rural reconstruction unit plan, stressed by Dr. Butterfield in his recent visits to Asia and Africa and in consultation with Christian leaders in the West, should, with any necessary adaptations, be tried out and extended in the different fields. This plan was defined as follows at the All-India Conference on Rural Work in Poona, India, which was held in April, 1930, in connection with his visit:

"A rural reconstruction unit is a group of contiguous villages, perhaps ten to fifteen in number, in which as full a program as possible of rural reconstruction service shall be made available to all the people. All agencies for educational, health, economic, and social progress will be urged to pool their efforts through some form of community council in an attempt to get the people to coöperate in building a new type of Indian rural community. The Church must lead this endeavor to make the enterprise thoroughly Christian in spirit. . . .

"It is our considered judgment that the creation of rural reconstruction units having their roots in the great human interests of the church, the school, the home, the hospital, and the bank and reaching out in the spirit of Christ through coöperation to serve the religious, educational, medical, social, and economic needs of all the rural people should be the united policy of missions and churches, and that the National Christian Council should do everything in its power to further such a policy." [2]

The full treatment of this plan, which may better be characterized, perhaps, as the rural community unit plan, and the more detailed findings on the subject, as given in *The Christian Mission in Rural India* by Dr. Butterfield, may well be made the subject of special study by groups in different countries who seek to develop such a fruitful plan for their respective fields. [3] The plan has the great merit of combining the all-too-meager and divided Protestant forces and bringing their united impact to bear upon a common problem. This concentration is in the interest of economy and efficiency. With adaptations it is widely reproducible.

5. On every considerable rural field special Christian rural institutions or rural departments of general Christian colleges or universities should be developed, together with adequate facilities for experimental work. Good examples of Christian institutions given up exclusively to training Christian rural workers are the Agricultural Institute near Allahabad, India, and the Lavras Agricultural College in Brazil. Among the

[2] Kenyon L. Butterfield, *The Christian Mission in Rural India: Report and Recommendations*, pp. 136 f., 141 (New York: The International Missionary Council, 1930). Copyright. Used by permission.

[3] Dr. Butterfield will issue in the autumn of the present year, 1931, a similar report on his visit to the countries of the Far East. This should be read in conjunction with his document on India.

best examples of agricultural departments are those of the Christian University of Nanking and Lingnan University in China, and that of Alwaye College in Travancore, India. These and similar institutions elsewhere should be much more liberally supported financially, and a number of the very best equipped men of Europe and America should be added to their staffs. In countries with large rural populations but not provided with such training facilities similar institutions or departments should be established. Theological seminaries should wherever practicable provide vocational courses for prospective rural pastors, and summer or winter vacation schools or training conferences should be developed to deal with the particular problems of rural pastors. This point of policy is of basic importance. It is not so much the number of leaders that one has in view as the fact that there simply must be at least a limited group trained and put in action each year who, in up-to-date equipment, and in ability to do creative work and to afford a real lead, will compare favorably with the very best men in the medical, industrial, and theological fields. Indeed, the task of preparing a sufficient supply of adequately prepared rural Christian workers for these great populations, both full-time paid leaders and an even larger number of volunteer local leaders, is of such magnitude and of such vital importance that it needs to be studied afresh both as to resources and as to method. Probably radical changes in content of cur-

riculum and in training technique, as well as far greater facilities, will be found necessary.

6. Steps should be taken to enlist more largely the
coöperation of universities, agricultural colleges, theological seminaries, and other institutions of North America and Europe where candidates for the missionary
career may best prepare themselves for their life work.
Each year hundreds of new missionaries are sent out
by European and American mission boards. Among
them are some who are planning to be agricultural missionaries and others who as regular missionaries expect
to work in rural communities. Both these classes should
receive specialized training to enable them to minister
to rural needs, just as intending educational and medical missionaries, in addition to their general education,
secure special training. Moreover, each year thousands
of missionaries come home on furlough, and many of
them desire to avail themselves of opportunities for advanced study which will qualify them to deal more effectively with rural problems. The nationals of the
Asiatic, Latin American, and African countries are increasingly coming to America and Europe for such
special vocational studies. Already a number of institutions in the West, such as the New York State College of Agriculture at Cornell University, Teachers College at Columbia University, and Tuskegee Institute in
Alabama, have arranged their regular and special
courses with reference to meeting these important needs

and demands. A manual is now in preparation which will give full information regarding the courses of study and other facilities afforded by the educational institutions and other organizations in North America for the guidance of mission boards, missionary candidates, and missionaries on furlough. It is hoped that in due time a document showing similar opportunities in the British Isles, Denmark, and certain other European countries may be issued.

7. There is need of multiplying greatly in the near future pieces of rural work which, because of their high quality, may serve as demonstration centers. Good illustrations are the truly notable village educational work at Moga, India; the Village of the New Day at Asansol, India; the Y. M. C. A. Center at Coimbatore, South India; the demonstration stations related to Nanking University; the varied rural activities of the Omi Mission in Japan; Kagawa's Peasant Gospel Schools in Japan; a Y. M. C. A. program in a typical area in Korea; also the Bunster Farm School at Angol, Chile; and the valuable work at such African centers as Old Umtali, Kambini, and Mount Silinda. Happily such examples are multiplying in different parts of the world, and if they are made more widely known, are sure to become contagious in their influence. *The Rural Billion,* the current textbook of the Missionary Education Movement, abounds in most interesting and telling illustrations of this kind.

8. Has not the time come when at least each of the larger mission boards should add to its headquarters staff a man or woman specially qualified and equipped to deal with the whole range of rural problems? Such a worker should be a man with rural consciousness, with some background of experience and training in agriculture, and in touch with recent developments in the field of rural uplift. No one step can be taken which will do more to insure that the claims of rural missions have their proper place in the thought, plans, and actions of the members and constituency of the boards, and that a truly worthy program be wrought out and executed.

Attention should be called to the invaluable service rendered by the International Association of Agricultural Missions, organized as a result of the timely initiative of Mr. Hunnicut of Brazil and backed effectively by other agricultural missionaries. It has represented both foreign and home mission boards of North America, and has called out notable contributions from many recognized authorities on rural work. The series of conferences held under its auspices and its other activities have done much to give the whole subject a more nearly central place in the thought of the churches. Some of its leaders have recognized the need of a supplementary agency to work in full coöperation. In collaboration with others, therefore, they are taking steps to develop a simple interdenominational body, to be known by some such designation as the Agricultural Missions Foundation or Council, designed to serve all the boards in matters of common concern, such as research, publications, visits of experts desired by the representatives of various boards at work in the same areas, fellowships for nationals for advanced study abroad, and the fostering of plans for united training. The devices suggested thus far should not, however, be substituted for the part which missions, mission boards, and their secretaries, and the churches both at home and in the field should take in a vigorous and aggressive support of a greatly enlarged work in the villages. The Church of the West should be made to understand that coöperation is vital in a new appeal and a new approach in missionary service and giving. For example, the appalling needs of the village women of these great continents constitute a call for both personnel and funds that should stir the hearts and secure the response of the womanhood of the West.

9. The deeper spiritual motive, meaning, and possibilities of the rural work should be stressed. Nowhere has this emphasis been made with finer insight and sympathy than by Dean John H. Reisner of the Agricultural College in Nanking, China, in an informal statement submitted to a group of representatives of agricultural colleges and of other laymen:

"Over and above all, the agricultural missionaries must make their work count toward a fuller knowledge and better understanding of God and toward an appreciation on the part of the farmer of the great fact that in performing one of the very greatest services to mankind in the production of food he is in a very real partnership with God. The agricultural missionaries must provide opportunities for Christian services that shall help men to enter into the Spirit of our Master who went about doing good, so that agriculture may be permeated with Christian ideals of service. They must make the Church the center of their thoughts and activities. . . .

"The great implications of agricultural missions are to my mind on the spiritual side. The great rural populations of such countries as India, China, Japan, and Korea cannot, in light of limited physical resources and mounting populations, have a great many things to live *with*, and what lasting satisfactions they have in life will in no small measure have to be derived from the things they are able to live *by*. I am referring particularly to the intangibles of rural life. If for us here in rural America where we have, relatively speaking, so many, many things to live with, it is difficult to secure contentment and satisfaction in rural life, how much more difficult in these countries of overpopulation and of relative poverty. The agricultural missionary will want to supplement rural evangelistic efforts with Christian services which can be carried out by the rural church and its members and which will show forth the Spirit of the Saviour and relate salvation to the whole life of the community. He will want to search for until he discovers the intangibles in the rural life of the community in which he is working and relate them consciously to the purposes of God. The country people are religious; their many gods represent to them powers in which they place their faith by worship. Much of their polytheistic worship has grown out of the economic need, and inasmuch as agriculture has largely provided the basis for their economic life many of their gods and superstitions are related to agricultural production and rural life. The farmer's life is surrounded by manifestations of God, many of which the farmer recognizes though lacking in understanding of them. These country people, steeped for centuries in superstitious lore, constitute great spiritual and religious reservoirs that must be tapped for God. Here to my mind are the greatest opportunities for service by agricultural missionaries, both men and women, and it is this field of the spirit in which they should make their greatest contributions in building up a rural civilization throughout the world which shall be Christian to the core."

Notwithstanding the many and great benefits which have been brought to Asia, Africa, and Latin America by the machine age, there have been associated with the spread of Western industrialism to these areas certain perils and evils which present a tremendous challenge to the world mission of Christianity. Expressed quite simply, the challenge to the Christian forces the world over is to act promptly and with all their power in order to save the peoples of these other continents from the disastrous results of mechanized civilization in the West. The conditions and practices which still obtain in parts of the Western countries are a shame and a reproach. All too late the churches in the West awakened to the dangers of the machine age in their own ranks, and only comparatively recently have even a limited number addressed themselves with any marked degree of understanding and conviction to bringing this vast and potent area under the sway of the principles and spirit of Christ. To-day economic questions occupy the minds of Christian leaders—both laymen and clergymen. In recent times they have come to recognize that economic troubles are of world-wide concern, and must be dealt with in a world context. For the first time in any widely general sense the world knows that it is an economic unity.

It is well that Christians of the West remind themselves that a very special burden of responsibility rests upon them to help their brothers in the Orient and Africa to meet the impending and already present dangers because these dangers have attended the spread of the industrialism of the West. In some respects this should be of special concern to American Christians because of the rapid introduction in recent years of the American type of industrial system—namely, that characterized by mass-production, scientific management, standardization, elimination of waste, and concentration of all available forces upon higher productivity.

This process of industrialization has been gathering momentum at a startling rate in recent decades. Within the lifetime of many now living, Japan, for example, has been transformed from an agricultural nation into one pronouncedly industrial. The process has been accelerated, notably since the Russo-Japanese War, because of the requirements of her congested and rapidly growing population. Her manufacturing cities now remind one of Manchester and Pittsburgh. It is estimated that over one-third of her population is in some way connected with industry. This development has been not only extensive but also progressive and efficient.

While India is a predominatingly rural field, according to the League of Nations' classification she is one of the eight leading industrial countries of the world. This has reference not only to her village or household industries, but also to the strength of her modern industrial establishments, such as the cotton mills of Western and Central India, the jute factories in Bengal, and the coal and iron works.

Notwithstanding the unsettled conditions in China, there has been somewhat remarkable modern industrial progress, especially in the Shanghai area and at other Yangtse points. This has been stimulated by the war and by the anti-Japanese boycott. Even in the midst of civil war conditions hundreds of new factories have been added. It is reported that the number of cotton spindles in five years increased from less than one million to over four millions. The vast untapped material resources, the abundant and cheap labor supply, and the almost boundless home market give promise of great developments in the next decade or two. China is destined to become a powerful competitor for the world industrial market. Thousands of Chinese students have been studying in the West preparing themselves to take important parts in the fields of manufacturing, mining, architecture, and commerce.

Taking the Oriental world as a whole, it may be said that the spread of Western industrialism has already had effects more far-reaching than the World

War. It has set in motion in the economic, social, and educational fields changes possibly quite as revolutionary as those in the sphere of political ideas.

For years great economic and social changes have been in progress among the peoples of South Africa in connection with the exploitation of the gold and diamond fields. In the Congo the industrial developments of recent years have been truly revolutionary in character and unprecedented in extent, depth, and rapidity. This is graphically set forth by Dr. Emory Ross:

"Nowhere in the world's history has so advanced a civilization made so rapid an impact upon so backward a people in so vast an area as in the present case of the Belgian Congo.

"Upon a country of people centuries retarded religiously, socially, and economically, among the most primitive in the world, has been thrust in two decades the fullest weight of all Occidental invention, organization, manufacture, commerce, transportation, acquisitiveness.

"The dense barriers of equatorial forests between village and village, tribe and tribe, have been broken through. Men, women, and infants who never before had been more than a day's walk from their village, have been transported in masses thousands of miles on conveyances never before seen, to work never before imagined, in the midst of conditions and laws never before experienced. . . .

"In the Katanga enormous gashes are cut in the earth by bewildered labor battalions under the shadow of huge machinery to get half the world's cobalt, the second largest amount of copper, and twenty grammes of the earth's yield of radium. In the Kasai, rivers are strained and the earth's surface is sifted to obtain the second largest output of diamonds. In the Ituri, mountains are tunneled like ant hills to bring forth five tons of gold each year.

"On the vast extent of waterways, where only lumpy, slow

canoes had gone, are fleets of giant steamers carrying with their tows a thousand times the charge of one canoe. Motor boats and hydrogliders multiply by twenty the speed of water travel. Railways lead in every direction. Motor roads allow ten-ton trucks to replace the porter with his fifty pounds. Overhead flies the greatest airfleet in Africa, which next year is also to link Congo with Europe. Telephone, telegraph, and wireless annihilate distance. . . .

"To the Congo native the total effect of all this is stupefying. He cannot take it in. Neither could any other folk, color entirely aside, if it had been all dropped down upon them in a short generation. Fifty years ago the whole Congo was absolutely unknown, untouched. For thirty years thereafter penetration was slow and slight. But during the past twenty years, and especially since the World War, it has been spectacular, overwhelming, unbelievable. . . . Only a small fraction of one per cent are enabled even to begin the immense readjustment necessary. For ten or eleven millions everything is simply uprooted. Anchor chains are parting, and nothing seems to hold. Increasing hundreds of thousands are definitely adrift." [1]

This world-wide spread of Western industry which has characterized our day has been attended with some extremely unfavorable results. It has brought with tenfold intensity upon the less highly organized lands and races of Asia and Africa most of the problems and perils which we have experienced on both sides of the Atlantic in the evolution of our industrial life and system. Bad as have been the consequences in the West, they have been much more serious in these other areas of the world because of the startling and bewildering rapidity of the movement, and the lack of any adequate

[1] Emory Ross, in *World Dominion, an International Review of Christian Progress*, Vol. VIII, No. 2, April, 1930, pp. 162 f.

Christian effort to meet the situation. What with us has been an evolution of generations, with them is being crowded into decades. Under the influence of the superior equipment and vast financial power of the West, and at times through its military might, the process has been speeded up, and orderly economic development has been impossible. It is not surprising, therefore, that some of the evils from which we of the West are as yet by no means free have come upon them.

Child labor is widely prevalent, and in some instances carried to greater extremes than in the West in its darkest days. Notwithstanding recent improvements and forward-looking plans of the government, the following observations made by Miss Margaret E. Burton, a careful student of conditions, after inspecting a factory near Shanghai, would still afford an unexaggerated picture of conditions in many an Asiatic center of industry:

"It was what is called a typical November day outdoors, with a raw chill that penetrated to the marrow. Inside the silk filature the atmosphere was like India in the monsoon, a sticky humid heat that covered spectacles with steam and made breathing a little difficult at first. One of the long row of small persons who were standing in front of the kettles of steaming water, brushing the silk cocoons for the women who were unwinding them, caught the visitor's eye. In the first place she was so very small, and in the second she looked so very old, working with a speed and concentration which were uncannily unchildlike. She was seven, Chinese count, the woman working opposite her said, which is six, even five, as we measure age. She came at five in the morning and left at seven in the evening, and she received ten cents a day. It was excellent pay for a child, the owner of the silk filature stated with pride. . . .

"Children are so helpless, so powerless to protect themselves from exploitation, that the terrible effect of China's new industrialism upon them may tend to blind us to what it is doing to older folk. But where such conditions of child labor exist, one can be sure that human life at every age is held cheap. No better description of the situation in China has been given than the terse statement that . . . conditions for men, women, and children [are] such as existed at the beginning of the industrial revolution in England one hundred and twenty-five years ago. Such labor regulations as the government issued in 1923 are quite impossible of enforcement under present conditions. Each factory is therefore a law unto itself. It may pay any wages, demand any number of hours of work, employ at any age, surround its workers with any kind of conditions, offer what it chooses in rest days and protection from accidents. There are progressive, open-minded employers who are aware of these evils and are sincerely desirous of making things better. There are outstanding examples of firms, such as the well-known Commercial Press of Shanghai, and many of the hair-net and lace factories of Chefoo, several of them owned and operated by Chinese Christians, in which the employers are honestly seeking the welfare of the workers. But it must be admitted that the cases in which wages, hours, and working conditions are even fairly good are lamentably few." [2]

There is also, as in the West, very extensive use of women in industry. As a rule the conditions are much more distressing than those which obtain in the West. In Japan, for example, nearly one-third of the workers in the mines are women, and their lot is tragic. It is

[2] Margaret E. Burton, *New Paths for Old Purposes*, pp. 27, 33 f. (New York: The Missionary Education Movement and Council of Women for Home Missions, 1927). Copyright. Used by permission.

said that the condition of the more than 2,000,000 women working in spinning factories is also very needy. In India 16 per cent of the factory workers are women. To afford a vivid realization of their hardships I quote again from Miss Burton:

"Probably nowhere in the world is the old adage, 'Man's work is from sun to sun, but woman's work is never done,' more true than among the factory workers of India. Long before dawn the woman who works must rise and grind the meal for her own and her family's breakfast. As soon as this is done she must make a trip to the nearest well, and take her place in the line, usually a long one, of women who are waiting to draw water. Then breakfast must be cooked and eaten, and additional food prepared and tied up ready to be taken to the factory. All this must be finished before half-past five at least, for most of the mills open at about six in the morning, and unless the workers live on the premises they may have two or three miles to walk.

"Frequently the woman makes this walk with her baby in her arms, the father carrying the next-to-youngest. Arrived at the mill, the mother tucks her baby away somewhere within reach and begins her ten hours of steady work, interrupted only by occasional care of the baby or of children a little older who run in and out, and an occasional break to eat. The intense heat, the clang of the machinery, which is so deafening that it is almost impossible to hear a word, the whirring wheels, which seem a constant menace to the unwary, and especially to the children, all contribute to an unceasing strain. At the end of ten hours of this the woman starts home again, where there is more meal to grind, more water to fetch, more hungry folk to feed, before she can rest. . . .

"The death rate among babies is probably higher in Bombay, the center of India's cotton industry, than anywhere in the world. Three-fourths of the babies of the factory workers in Bombay are said to be born in one-room tenements. More than a fifth of these single-room tenements are occupied by from six to nine people, and many have ten or more occupants. A floor space of ten feet by ten is a very common measurement. Add to this the common use of opium for babies, the stifling and fluff-laden air of the mills in which they spend their days, and, not least, the effect of excessive work under bad conditions both in mill and tenement upon the mother's vitality, and one can find no cause for surprise at the fact that one of every two babies dies before reaching the age of a year." [3]

Attention must also be called to the fact that so much of the labor in connection with modern industries is underpaid. Though this is still true in parts of the Western world, far greater inequalities and injustices obtain in Africa and Asia. With an almost negligibly small number of exceptions men, women, and children are miserably underpaid, a vastly disproportionate share of the profits of the industrial concerns going to owners and stockholders. The wide differences in standards of living are regarded by some of the ablest students of world affairs as constituting a great menace to international peace and good will. Not long ago a certain Chinese manufacturing company, desiring more capital, advertised the business as follows:

"The profits last year surpassed $1,000,000. For the past two years it has been running night and day with scarcely any intermission. The number of hands employed is 2,500, and the following is the wage table per day:

"Men, 15 to 25 cents; women, 10 to 15 cents; boys about 15 years, 10 to 15 cents; girls about 15 years, 5 to 10 cents; small boys and girls under 10 years, from $3\frac{1}{2}$ to 10 cents.

"The working hours are from five-thirty in the morning

[3] *Ibid.*, pp. 48 f., 51.

until five-thirty in the evening, and from five-thirty in the evening until five-thirty in the morning. No meals are supplied by the factory.

"It will be seen that the company is in an exceptionally favorable condition, with an abundant supply of cheap labor to draw from. The annual profits have exceeded the total capital on at least three occasions."

There is growing complaint that in the exploitation by Western industry of the vast natural resources of gold, copper, cobalt, rubber, cotton, silk, sugar, and other products the workmen who are native to the country are not beginning to receive their proper share. Those who thus complain have in mind not only the totally inadequate wages of the working men and working women, but also the fact that so small a portion of the vast profits of the industry is devoted to the betterment of the inhabitants and the upbuilding of the country. Such policies and practices are exceedingly short-sighted even from a business point of view. An acute observer in South Africa, commenting on the fact that since 1868 the total amount of gold produced in that country was nearly £1,000,000,000, asked the searching question, "What did the African get from this exploitation of the wealth of his country?" In answer to his own question he maintains, "Long hours, pitiably inadequate wages, inhuman sanitary conditions, accidents without proper compensation, disintegration of family life, racial bitterness and strife."

One of the most serious consequences of the spread

of Western industry in so many parts of Asia, as well as
of South and Central Africa, has been the break-up of
family and tribal life, customs, and traditions. Millions of men and women are taken from their houses in
the villages and brought to live for long periods in the
midst of unhealthful conditions in or near the great
centers of industry. The effect on the home life and
the welfare of the children is ruinous, for seldom is
urban life so favorable as normal life back on the land
or in the village. For example, nearly 500,000 Bantu
workers have been brought from all parts of South
Africa and massed in and near Johannesburg in what
is virtually a vast concentration camp. There is little to
counteract the downward pull of the fierce temptations
which beset them. The conditions of the slums are reproduced. Vice is rampant. Lawlessness is prevalent.
The friction points between whites and blacks are multiplied and aggravated. The rate of mortality is shock-
ingly high. A delegate at the Jerusalem conference
told of 240 young men dying out of one unit of 1,000
within the first year after they left their village homes.
This confirms what General Smuts predicted years ago
when, in a speech in Parliament, he emphasized that
"the future difficulties will not be with the raw native
in his village but in the great centers where are con-
gregating hundreds of thousands of these people."

The immemorial system of handicraft or domestic
industries has fast been giving way in the Orient before

the invasion of Western machinery and the modern factory system. The novelty and the cheapness of the new product drive out the old. Any who have had intimate acquaintance with the originality, individuality, richness, and æsthetic quality of much of the old work cannot but deplore what is taking place. This is after making generous allowance for compensating benefits of the modern system. We cannot lose sight of the fact that invaluable home crafts are being destroyed, that in countless instances workers have been thrown out of employment, and that influences have been set in motion which, as has been pointed out, have markedly weakened family solidarity and well-being.

In face of results like these one can understand why Gandhi, in the light of what he has witnessed in India and South Africa, not to mention Europe, speaks of the influences of Western industrialism as sinister and diabolical, and that with passionate effort by voice and pen, in season and out of season, he strives to turn back its tide and to perpetuate homespun and handicraft. Of course this tide can no more be stayed than that of the sea. It is recognized, however, that it must be brought under proper control, and its powers directed to unselfish, constructive ends. It is equally important to realize that there is very great urgency in the present situation, if we are to avert in Africa and the East the grave dangers and sins which in the modern age have attended the development of the industrial life of the

West. In forcing open Asia and taking possession of Africa the West has taken upon itself not only an overwhelming world problem but also a most solemnizing responsibility. Professor Buell reminds us that the white man is free and able to avoid, for example, in South and Central Africa, mistakes such as he has committed in the past in other parts of the world "if he has the will and intelligence to do it." But he has no time to lose.

The central question is whether the rest of the world is to travel the economic path of the West, or whether, with our coöperation, it shall profit from our unfortunate experiences of inequality, injustice, class hatred, destructive communism, and strife, and chart a new course for mankind in industrial life and relations. Prompt, statesmanlike action on the part of agencies and individuals who are in a position to render effective assistance may not only do much to break the force of evils which our Western industrial system has visited upon these other continents but also eventually establish there a social organization and life free from many defects of our own.

On the Christian forces of the West rests a unique, heavy, and unescapable responsibility for taking the initiative and leadership in meeting this grave and emergent situation. If they do not help to provide the solution, industrialism may ultimately prevent the Church from wielding any effective influence in these

lands. Instead of regarding this situation with indifference or with a sense of powerlessness, and address-
ing itself to the task with half-heartedness, the Church
should, with unshakable confidence and contagious faith,
strive to meet this challenge to humanize industry by
bringing it under the sway of Christ. Only His program and His power are adequate to meet the challenge.
His Gospel is intended not only to satisfy the deepest
needs and highest aspirations of the individual soul,
but also to make possible the creation of the society
and the insuring of economic relations in which individual men as members of a spiritual brotherhood can
live the abundant life. His guiding principles of the
infinite worth of human personality, of brotherhood,
and of corporate responsibility will not fail. As Christians we cannot escape the moral responsibility for applying these principles. If the world mission fails at
this point, its message will lose its validity in the thought
of non-Christians in touch with the tragic facts of the
spread of industrialism. To foster the outworking of
these unerring principles will help remove the stumblingblock caused by unchristian attitudes and acts associated
with the industrial impact of nominally Christian lands.

Notwithstanding the general unresponsiveness to the
stern challenge of this industrial situation, an unresponsiveness due to lack of awareness of the facts and their
implications, there are multiplying evidences of growing solicitude of Christians in all parts of the world.

This is particularly noticeable in the leaders of the world mission of Christianity both in the countries which have been sending out missionaries and in those to which the missionaries have been sent. The discussions at the Stockholm Conference on Life and Work and the deliverances of the recent Copec Conference in England dealt with those aspects of the problem which specially concern the situation in Western countries. It was at the Meeting of the International Missionary Council at Jerusalem that the subject was for the first time lifted up into a place of central prominence as a world problem. Under the guidance of prophetic leaders, such as Professor Tawney of the London School of Economics, the late Mr. Harold Grimshaw of the International Labor Office, and Bishop Francis J. McConnell of New York, and with the collaboration of trusted observers and thinkers who had come from face-to-face contacts with the facts in the inflamed industrial zones of the different continents, a masterly diagnosis of the problem was made and a constructive program was wrought out. The entire conference participated in the unhurried consideration of the question. This emphasis stands out in striking contrast with that of the preceding World Missionary Conference, held in Edinburgh in 1910, where during the entire ten days of sessions of the largest, most representative gathering of its kind held up to that time, the subject of industrial life and relationships was scarcely mentioned.

Nothing can better indicate the evolution in the thinking, the shifting of the stress, and the widening of the program of Christian leaders of modern times. Jerusalem has furnished the much-needed sounding board and broadcasting station which has made possible arresting the attention, quickening the conscience, and stimulating the will of Christians the world over in reference to this great area of human need sinful neglect, and Christian obligation.

The following constructive measures are suggested to meet these impending dangers:

1. The leaders of all the Christian forces related to the world mission might well take as their own the guiding principles and objectives adopted by the Jerusalem conference set forth in Volume V of the printed report.

2. Every backing should be given to the Department of Social and Industrial Research and Counsel established by the International Missionary Council at the recent Jerusalem Meeting. This Department has its headquarters at Geneva, where it can avail itself of the priceless contacts and facilities afforded by the League of Nations, the International Labor Office, the World's Student Christian Federation, the Stockholm Conference Continuation Committee, the World's Y. M. C. A., the World's Y. W. C. A., and many other international bodies. The access and coöperation thus made possible will not only effect great savings financially but will also insure great enrichment of program and facility in car-

rying out policies. The coöperation of all these agencies is assured. The functions of the Department are:

a. To produce reports and supply information on the economic and social problems arising from the contact between more advanced economic civilizations and the peoples of undeveloped countries, and to this end to secure that the necessary research is regularly undertaken.

b. To influence public opinion in various countries in regard to their responsibility for conditions which obtain in certain other areas of the world.

c. To advise the missionary organizations as to the special economic and social problems of the areas in which they are working.

d. To arrange for joint action between different Christian bodies, both in sending countries and on the mission field, with a view to the removal of unchristian conditions of life and work.

e. To bring to the notice of Christian bodies and mission boards the urgent necessity of securing an adequate supply of competent workers in the mission field equipped with the necessary economic and social training.

f. To bring to the notice of Christian bodies and missionaries the importance (1) of forming groups of students who will investigate social and economic problems in their various areas and disseminate knowledge of them, and (2) of emphasizing in their schools and other educational activities the social content of the Christian message.

g. To coöperate with other agencies, both public and private, in all measures which have as their object to raise the level of economic and social life.

The Council has been fortunate in securing for the executive officers of this department Mr. J. Merle Davis, for many years a missionary in Japan, where he specialized in industrial problems, and later for six years the pioneer General Secretary of the Institute of Pacific Relations, and Dr. Otto Iserland, of Germany, who also has had educational experience in the Orient and has devoted years to the special study of economics in Europe and America. Already they have received so many demands for their services that they are involved in a constant study of priorities to determine which claims and projects should have right of way. It is evident that the help of leading authorities will have to be enlisted on various aspects of the problems in the industrial area. It is believed also that all necessary funds will be forthcoming from wise donors who will recognize in this undertaking, which involves uniting the best thought and the most influential action of all nations and Christian communions and bringing them to bear upon one of the greatest world issues confronting Christendom, one of the most highly useful and productive uses of money.

3. What has already been said about coöperation

with this new organ of the world mission suggests the desirability, in fact the necessity, of achieving a larger synthesis of constructive forces. In such dealing with an issue of world-wide extent and concern, involving so many relationships and, at times, such highly specialized knowledge, the unofficial coöperation, at least, of other organizations and movements of an altruistic and constructive character will greatly facilitate the realization of the ends in view. A good illustration is that of the International Labor Office. What does not the cause of Christian missions owe to the counsel so freely given by Mr. Grimshaw, one of its ablest executives, both at Jerusalem and in the many consultations when the policy of the new department was being worked out. His premature death has been an irreparable loss to this great cause.

4. Each national Christian council in the lands of the younger churches, such as Japan, Korea, China, the Philippines, the Netherlands Indies, India, Burma, and Ceylon, Latin America, the Near East and Northern Africa, the Congo, South Africa, and other sections of Africa where similar bodies are being developed, should increasingly take this industrial problem into its purview and practical program. In the fields where there has already been a marked expansion or impact of Western industrialism the national council should set up a competent committee to specialize in industrial fields and relations, and in some countries, such as China, In-

dia, Japan, and the Congo, it will doubtless be desirable
to set apart one or more workers to give their whole
time to meeting the claims of the situation as representative of all the churches and missions. In China such
provision has already been made, and a real leadership
is being afforded with gratifying results. This is the
voice of experience in the countries where most satisfactory progress has been achieved. An industrial program for a national council in a typical field of expanding modern industrialism might well include such features as these:

a. Research work, *e.g.*, the copper mining fields of
the Southern Congo.

b. An information bureau on Christian experience
and plans in industrial work throughout the country, and
on the most helpful experiences of other countries.

c. Conducting an educational campaign among the
indigenous churches of the country, through addresses,
study circles, use of literature, inspection of fruitful
pieces of work.

d. Training institutes or courses for intensive preparation of workers, both pastors and laymen, in industrial
areas.

e. Establishing welfare service units in industrial
fields in or near which two or more denominations are
at work (including a simple building, a paid or volunteer worker in charge, reading room, education facilities

for adults, musical facilities, scouting, free medical advice, and free legal help).

f. Establishing one or more model villages for industrial workers and their families like the one under the Y. M. C. A. among the cotton-mill operatives at Nagpur, India.

g. Vocational education to help the unemployed and those who are working unproductively.

h. Fostering existing village industries, also discovering and introducing suitable supplementary industries, as has been done in Korea, India, and China.

i. Introducing coöperative societies for purchasing, marketing, and other purposes.

j. Effecting correlation between such industrial service units and rural reconstruction units.

k. Enlisting the help of colleges and universities, both those under Christian and those under government auspices, to further the preparation of efficient workers.

l. Influencing government legislation in the interest of 'the welfare of working men and working women, having in view the standards emphasized by the International Labor Office.

m. Establishing mutual aid societies among workers in industry, as advocated by Dr. Kagawa of Japan.

n. Above all, bringing about fruitful coöperation in thinking, planning, intercession, and action among all the Christian forces of the country.

5. The corresponding bodies in the countries which

send missionaries, such as the Standing Committee of the Missionary Societies of Great Britain and Ireland and the Committee of Reference and Counsel of the United States and Canada, should also assign a very able and specially qualified group of the best men and women of the country, to give central direction to the studying, policy-making, and coöperative action of the various mission boards and church constituencies seeking to make greatly needed and worth-while contributions toward the solution of the industrial problems. Functions similar to those outlined above for councils in lands to which missionaries are sent, with necessary adaptations, will at once suggest themselves. If really great results so imperatively needed in grappling successfully with the most difficult and emergent problems of the industrial area are to be secured, there must be an adequate cause. It is believed, in the light of experience, that the most efficient cause is a group of creative, courageous spirits with a definite and heavy burden of responsibility placed upon them and working in conscious reliance upon the assured help of the Ever-Living and Ever-Creative God.

6. Each mission board of Europe and North America having work in modern industrial areas should encourage its representatives on the field to work out, in collaboration with the churches to which they are related, definite programs and policies, and should do all in their power to make possible the giving effect to those

plans. To this end new missionaries who are to serve in such fields should, in addition to their general preparation, be given supplemental training with reference to meeting the demands of the industrial work. As we recall the quality and specialized training of the great pioneer medical missionaries and of the educational missionaries who did the most enduring foundation work, we recognize the wisdom of exercising like care in the selection and equipping of those who are to set right precedents in this very neglected and highly important field. Just how great the neglect has been may be seen in the fact that it is difficult to discover even a score of men and women in all the industrial areas of the so-called non-Christian world who are devoting themselves exclusively to the industrial problem, and not half of these, so far as can be learned, had received special preparation for the task of humanizing and Christianizing industrial conditions and relations.

7. If the vitally important objective, that of having this new area of life brought under Christ's sway, is to be realized, there are a few basic needs which must be met:

Chief attention must be concentrated on dealing with the causes of existing injustices, cruelties, ill will, and other unchristian facts and conditions. Not dealing with the wounded but seeking to stop the fight must be the main concern.

Prayer and diligent search must be brought to bear

to multiply the number of prophetic utterances devoted to quickening the conscience and energizing the will for sacrificial action among the members of the older churches of the West and the younger churches of Asia, Africa, and Latin America. Great is the need of penetrating thinkers, wise interpreters, and truly prophetic dynamic advocates for this all-too-neglected cause.

Warriors also are imperatively needed in the years immediately before us. Some of the cruelest wrongs of our day will not be righted without such heroic characters. Mr. Grimshaw was such a one. His report on forced labor in Africa presented at the International Labor Congress shortly before his death called for the highest order of heroism. In a session where it was being discussed a Roman Catholic priest rose and said, "Gentlemen, we should fall upon our knees and thank God for the man who had the honesty and courage to write that report." If the conscience of Christendom is to be made to tremble, men of the mold, courage, and sense of mission which characterized Old Testament prophets must be raised up.

The new generation must be captured for this cause. They need just such impossible tasks to call out their latent powers. Moreover, the cause needs them. The older generation will not live long enough to effect the extensive and profound changes which are demanded in this difficult and relatively unworked field, but the youth now within college walls will. To win them men and women who have had first-hand contacts with the zones of conflict in industry, like Ray E. Phillips of South Africa, Emory Ross of the Congo, C. F. Andrews of India, J. B. Tayler of China, Miss Agatha Harrison, formerly of China, and Miss Margaret Burton, should visit the colleges and seminaries and share their burdens and visions. Their words will not return void.

The nation-wide Kingdom of God Campaign now in progress in Japan under the leadership of the Christian social reformer, Dr. Kagawa, should be studied in the setting of this great world-wide issue. In its conception and conduct this movement reveals an awareness of the industrial issue and the critical aspect it presents in Japan, the most highly industrialized nation of the non-Christian world. It is also striking at the heart of the problem in every country. Kagawa's program is concrete and constructive and workable. It is reported that his two visits to China within the past year, where he presented a gospel which comprehended the need of China's industrial as well as her rural field, made a deep impression and called forth an instant response. It is a significant fact that his vision of a world-wide movement of social (as well as individual) evangelism came to him while, during the session of the Jerusalem conference, he was in prayer far away in Japan for that creative gathering. May it not be that the time is ripe in many a field for a like proclamation of a whole gospel?

In reality the faith of Christians is involved in the way in which they meet this great issue and challenge. Have we or have we not a Gospel adequate to meet the deepest need of this vast area of human need and neglect? Let Professor Tawney answer:

"You cannot at once preach the religion of Christianity and practice the religion of material success, which is the creed of a great part of the Western world and is the true competitor of Christianity for the allegiance of mankind. To divorce religion from the matters of social organization and economic activity which occupy nine-tenths of the life of nine-tenths of mankind, on the ground that they are common and unclean, is to make them unclean, and ultimately to destroy religion in the individual soul to which you have attempted to confine it.

"It must be the task of Christianity, I submit, to overcome that divorce. It must overcome it not in order to secularize the churches, but in order to spiritualize society. It is not a question of allowing economic interests to encroach on spiritual interests, but of dedicating man's struggle with nature, which is what, properly understood, his industry is, to the service of God, in order that it may no longer be a struggle with his fellow men. It is not a question of diluting the arduous claims of Christianity, but of asserting its right to conquer a new province. It is not a question of the Church's allying itself with this political party or that, but of its defining its own position and allowing political parties to adjust, as they think best, their own attitude to it. . . .

". . . The churches are neglecting an essential part of their mission unless they foster the zeal for social righteousness, and disseminate the knowledge by which such zeal may be made effective. It must be their task, by reaffirming the social application of their own principles, to point the way to a society in which men may enjoy not only material comfort but spiritual peace, because they feel that their social institutions and industrial organization are the expression not merely of economic expediency or convenience, but of justice." [4]

[4] R. H. Tawney, in *The Christian Mission in Relation to Industrial Problems.* The Jerusalem Meeting of the International Missionary Council, March 24–April 8, 1928, Vol. V, pp. 128 f., 131 (New York: The International Missionary Council, 1928). Copyright. Used by permission.

IV. THE SUMMONS OF RACE

THE RACE PROBLEM IS ONE OF world-wide interest and world-wide concern, involving not one race but all races. Its solution must, therefore, be worked out in a world context.

The race problem is also one of the greatest gravity. The shrinkage of the world, due largely to constant improvement in the means of communication, has set the races to acting and reacting upon each other with startling directness, power, and virulence. This is done through the movement of the tides of emigration and immigration, and also through modern world-ramifying industry, commerce, and finance, not to mention other important points or occasions of contact. There is a constant and growing mingling of peoples both on the higher and on the lower levels of life. A serious aspect of the matter is that wherever two or more races are brought into close contact, without the restraining influence of a power greater than human, demoralization usually follows. Something takes place when races meet which tends to draw out the worst in each race, as well as the best. There are in individuals of all races not only heights which reach up to heaven, but also depths which lay hold on hell. The deepest hell into which I have ever gazed has been in places where the races have been thrown against each other without moral and spiritual restraint. The war has greatly accentuated this peril as well as many others. Nations and races have awakened under the impulse of ideals of freedom and self-determination— ideals which came into marked prominence in the thought and feeling of the world during the great struggle and the subsequent international discussions. Be the causes what they may, the friction points between the races today are more numerous and also more inflamed than they were two decades ago. Some of the most alarming racial misunderstandings and clashes have taken place in the past few years. At once we all think of solemnizing examples in Africa, North and South, in different parts of North America, also in Eastern, Southern, and Western Asia. Europe, the base of so many colonial powers, has been and is most intimately concerned in these racial developments on the other continents. The world-wide situation may be characterized as one of distrust, irritation, and bitterness. Unmistakably there is a growing volume of racial animosity throughout the world. Dr. S. K. Datta, of India, in writing me on the subject, may have gone to an extreme, although many agree with him, in stating that there is "hardly any interracial trust and good will."

The racial problem of this day is indeed urgent. It is, as C. F. Andrews of India says, "the most immediate problem of our own times." This intensification is due to the greatly accelerated pace in the movements of mankind, to the startling development of divisive forces among the nations and races, and to the rapid spread of the corrupt influences of so-called Western civilization. Now that the world has found itself as one body, this critical situation cannot be a matter of indifference to any race or nation. We all agree that it has a very vital bearing on the missionary program. Even though we redouble our efforts, multiply our forces, and improve our methods and organization, we shall still be laboring under a most serious handicap if a widening chasm of mistrust yawns between us and those of other races whom we wish to reach.

The race problem is not without its inspiring aspects. Through it all is evident a movement of the higher spirit in man, a desire and hope of realizing a freer, fairer, and nobler future for all. We should also bear in mind the unmistakable purpose of the Heavenly Father to bring His entire human family into accord and unity. The very difficulties which beset the interracial situation present an added attraction. History shows that great issues and grave perils are required to develop great races and nations. The Christian religion, in particular, requires what, from the human point of view, is the impossible in order to afford demonstrations of its sufficiency and conquering power. One ground of my confidence that the Christian forces are on the threshold of something far greater and more wonderful than we have ever known is the fact that we find ourselves in the midst of an overwhelmingly difficult, even impossible, task.

Through the centuries solutions of the problem of race relations have been attempted. All of them have their advocates to-day. It is evident to all who have reflected on the subject that there can be no quick or easy way. What are some of those proposed and advocated? One might be characterized as that of domination or subjugation. This suggests the answer given by Sir Robert Hart, the eminent British civilian, for so many years at the head of the Imperial Customs in China, when I asked him how the race problem could be met. He indicated two alternatives. One, in which he evidently had no confidence, was "a colossal military and naval establishment—so colossal that it would break down the so-called powers of the world to maintain it." He saw, what I am sure we all see, that such an attempt would utterly fail, because it would tend to aggravate rather than relieve the very difficulty we wish to see overcome.

Others have insisted on a policy of segregation. If history has taught anything, however, it has been the impossibility of segregating completely, and, therefore, effectively, any race. If that has been true in the past, it is likely to be still more true in the period before us, in view of the far more complex, rapid, and irresistible interaction of peoples. While some nations, like America, Australia, and Canada, may have policies and legislation which prevent certain races from coming to them, they cannot, in this day of constantly improving communications, of industrial and commercial expansion, and of multiplying contacts in other departments of life, keep the aggressive elements of their own race from going forth to other parts of the world and mingling with other peoples. Thus inevitably the ideas, ideals, habits, and tendencies of one race will be brought to bear upon those of other races. Not a few leading minds, as well as large numbers of those who are not given to thinking these matters through, believe in what they call "racial and social segregation on the basis of equality of opportunity." Wherever tried it soon becomes evident that the first part of the formula contradicts or nullifies the second. Generally speaking, the Christian conscience of the world, so far as I know, does not rest upon segregation as the ultimate ideal or practice for the solution of the race problem. The Christian spirit is necessarily missionary and inclusive, and cannot be content to let any barriers permanently remain between man and man.

Some voices are questioning whether the world is not being driven to conclude that there must be a policy of federation of certain races, which would ultimately, for example, group the Orientals as against the Occidentals, or the whites as against the blacks, or the Jews as against the Gentiles. The arguments used, however, are not such as appeal to the higher levels in the realm of ideals.

In my judgment none of these solutions shows the pathway out of our difficulties. Through bitterness, strife, bloodshed, and failure we are being led to see Christ's way, the pathway of love, of human brotherhood and mutual service. Let me now refer to the alternative mentioned by Sir Robert Hart in that unforgettable conversation in Peking. His full answer was, "A colossal military and naval establishment—so colossal that it would break down the so-called powers of the world to maintain it—or the spread of Christianity in its purest form."

There are certain principles and teachings of Jesus Christ which, if applied to interracial relations, would, it is believed, flood the world increasingly with good will and unselfish action.

First among these is the teaching of the Fatherhood of God. Where, before Jesus came, was God proclaimed as the Father of all races and of all mankind, and who before Jesus illustrated God as a father as we now understand the term? Is it not true, also, that from the early ages, before Jesus came, men were asking the question, Am I my brother's keeper? Since He came and taught and illustrated, men in increasing numbers have been affirming, I am my brother's brother. We recognize that there is all the difference in the world in the effect of these Christlike conceptions on the problem of race relationships.

The infinite value of each race is likewise preëminently a Christian conception, as we can clearly see in contrasting what Jesus taught and did with reference to so-called despised peoples, with the attitude and action of the non-Christian religions, or of irreligion.

Each race has a unique contribution to make to our common civilization and to Christianity, and should have adequate opportunity to make its largest and best contribution. This truth was enforced by Christ in some of His most searching teachings and parables.

Yet another principle is that inequalities in races should not be made the occasion for domination or exploitation, but rather for the display of level justice, and, above all, for the rendering of service—service, in particular, by the strong or advanced races on behalf of the weak or backward races. In these days we hear and read a great deal about race superiority. It has been interesting to me to observe in my travels that virtually every race considers itself superior. Christ has indicated the only ground on which any race or individual can win superiority, "Whosoever would be first among you, shall be servant of all." Christ's teaching and attitude clearly show that all men and peoples are equal before God. He proclaimed to them one Gospel. His program summons His followers to make disciples on an equal spiritual footing of all races.

There is one kingdom over which He is to reign as the one Lord.

Another guiding principle is that the different races are members one of another, and, therefore, essential to one another. This alone, if applied, would soften racial asperities and usher in a new day.

The Golden Rule, also, is surely applicable between races as between individuals.

Then there is Christ's wonderful commandment of love—love not only to God but to man, the love of one's neighbor as one's self. What religion, save the Christian religion, has commanded that we love our enemies? Without doubt this commandment, if taken seriously and applied resolutely, would dissolve the race problem. In teaching as Christ did, that we are to love one another as He loved us, He left no ground for questioning as to His own mind on all that is involved in race relationships.

St. Paul realized the all-inclusiveness of Christ's vision and purpose when he proclaimed that "One is your Master, even Christ, and all ye are brethren." The more we ponder the fact of the universality of Christ and of Christ's program, the more its marvelous and satisfying interracial implications will impress themselves upon us.

We may all have a part in a practical working program to which Christians may lend themselves in the interest of insuring, through right racial relations, the gradual and ultimate solution of the racial problem:

1. Every Christian should seek to discover the mind of Christ on the subject of race relationships, and then make that mind his own. Without doubt this is the greatest single contribution which each one of us can make to the solution of the race problem. The attitude and spirit of Christ, revealed in His teachings regarding men and women of different races, as well as in His relationships to them, best indicate the attitude of mind and heart which we should develop and the practices which we should observe when this idea becomes a dominating personal purpose.

2. On every hand the serious study of the race problem should be promoted. No subject calls for more intense thinking, clearer thinking, and more unselfish thinking. In the first place, we should give ourselves to furthering the organization and able direction of study circles and open forums in universities, colleges, and schools, and among various groups in connection with our churches and other societies. Happily, there are in existence in different countries a number of well-prepared courses which may serve as the basis for such studies and discussions. One of the best pieces of work of this kind is the study of race relationships between the whites and blacks which has been in progress for a number of years among the white and Negro colleges and at the student conferences of both races in the

Southern States of America. This was first inaugurated among the white colleges, and some years as many as 5,000 students in these colleges engaged in intensive study of this particular aspect of the race problem. Later, similar circles were organized and conducted with like helpfulness in the colored colleges. This invaluable work has now been in progress so long that its effects are becoming increasingly apparent in all parts of the Southern States, notably in the direction of a well-informed, unselfish, and determined leadership of thought and action among men and women of both races to bring about the needed and desired improvement in race relationships.

Another illustration of scientific study of the race problem is the piece of research which was conducted a few years ago on the Pacific Coast of the United States and Canada, under the stimulus, and with the collaboration, of the Institute of Social and Religious Research. There were established in British Columbia, Canada, in the State of Washington, in the State of Oregon, and both in Central and in Southern California, representative commissions composed of men prominent in business affairs, professors, clergymen, labor leaders, and others, for the purpose of making first-hand studies of different aspects of the relations between Anglo-Saxons, on the one hand, and Orientals—East Indians, Japanese, and Chinese—on the other hand. The work of these separate commissions was under the supervision of a unifying group of leading minds, representing the entire Pacific Coast of North America. Though the extensive and intensive studies thus initiated were never fully completed, sufficient progress was made to justify the statement that this is one of the most constructive approaches to the study of the race problem which have thus far been undertaken.

Still another approach to the racial as well as other problems of a great area of the world is that presented by the Institute of Pacific Relations. It may be confidently predicted that such collaboration of thoughtful men and women in the part of the world where the racial problem has assumed such central importance will have a large influence in furthering right relations among the races of the Pacific.

3. The holding of intimate interracial conferences and retreats, with the racial problem definitely in mind, should be furthered. Here one has in mind carefully selected groups of influential Christians of the races concerned who will go apart to spend time in unhurried conference, in spiritual fellowship and united intercession to the end that a better understanding may be insured and more effective measures put into operation for promoting right race relationships. The recent conference of Bantu and European students held at Fort Hare in South Africa is a splendid example. Many interesting instances of intimate meetings of this kind which have been held since the war among Christian

leaders of different races in the Far East, in Europe, in North America, in South Africa, and in India might be given. It is significant that these widely separated meetings, having in view the same object, were held independently of one another and were in no sense initiated from a common source. It is also a striking fact that many more such gatherings have been held since the war than before. All this shows on the part of Christians a growing recognition of the increasing gravity of the racial problem and the purpose to bring more resolutely to bear upon it the Christian contribution.

4. Steps should be taken to utilize more fully the opportunities presented at representative international and world conferences. In some respects the conferences of the World's Student Christian Federation, notably those held at Peking, China, in 1922, and at Mysore, India, in 1928, have lent themselves best to this purpose. These gatherings afford unique opportunities to develop right atmosphere and to establish enduring friendships among those of the different races who are in a position to exert the most far-reaching influence.

5. We should introduce widely the most notable books bearing on race relations and stimulate the study of them. Among the most valuable for this purpose which have been issued within recent years are the following:

Christianity and the Race Problem, J. H. Oldham.

Race and Race Relations: A Christian View of Human Contacts, Robert E. Speer.

The Negro from Africa to America, W. D. Weatherford.

The Clash of Color, Basil Mathews.

And Who Is My Neighbor? Published by "The Inquiry," in America.

Education in East Africa, Thomas Jesse Jones.

Reports of the sessions of the Institute of Pacific Relations held in 1925, 1927, 1929.

The Teachings of Jesus on Human Relations, John S. Hoyland. (In England, *The Race Problem and the Teaching of Jesus Christ.*)

American Democracy and Asiatic Citizenship, Sidney L. Gulick.

The Relation of the Advanced and Backward Races of Mankind, James Bryce.

It is interesting to observe that nine of these works were written by Christians, and that the authors of seven of the number were former leaders of the student Christian movement in different parts of the world.

Other books of special significance are:

The Rising Tide of Color Against White World Supremacy, Lothrop Stoddard.

Asia and Europe, Meredith Townsend.

Up From Slavery, Booker T. Washington.

What the Negro Thinks, Robert Russa Moton.

Aggrey of Africa, Edwin W. Smith.

The Basis of Ascendancy, Edgar Gardner Murphy.

The Trend of the Races, George E. Haynes.

The Speeches and Writings of Gandhi.

The Real Japanese Question, K. K. Kawakami.

Kenya, Norman Leys.

6. A vital point, second in importance to none, is that each Christian who desires to help solve the race problem seek to make personal friends of individuals of different races. One of the principal causes of all the trouble is that too many are prone to think of the people of a race in the mass, and fail to individualize in a person, as Jesus Christ did. So long as a race is a mere abstraction we shall never understand or appreciate, whereas if we establish intimate friendship with individual members of races, we shall have keys that will help unlock the problem.

7. In this connection the value of having contacts with the home life of men of other races should be emphasized. This changes a man's whole outlook, disposition, and feeling on the matter. It serves as an absolutely invaluable corrective of impressions received from other sources. It acts as a restraining influence at times when racial feeling is running high. Think what a great and permanent unifying influence has resulted from the fact that Joseph Neesima, of Japan, as a schoolboy in America, was taken into the home of Mr. Hardy, educated by him, and treated almost as a son. The carrying out of this point of policy will result in breaking down increasingly, as nothing else can possibly do, the superiority complex with which races are so prone to think of each other. We can all recall sad examples of the opposite kind of influence exerted by men who, while living in other lands, were not ex-

posed to helpful influences or contacts with the home life of Christian people.

8. The program for promoting friendly relations among foreign students should be greatly enlarged. The campaign of friendship which has, during the past thirty years, been conducted with growing efficiency by certain student Christian movements on behalf of foreign students who have come among them, has been the most helpful single factor in furthering better permanent race relationships. Student migrations are increasing in many parts of the world. It is a movement which should be encouraged. A disproportionately large share of the leaders of to-morrow among the nations and races of mankind will continue to come from the young men and women who avail themselves of the unique advantages resulting from extended periods of thorough study in foreign lands. It should not be regarded as an impossible ideal and undertaking that the World's Student Christian Federation, with the coöperation of the national student Christian movements and of the various churches, should spread such an intimate network of friendly relations over all these many thousands who thus sojourn in foreign lands as to result in permanent understanding, good will, and coöperation. When such contacts are not provided, the inevitable result is the multiplication of the number of sad examples of the very opposite kind of influence exerted by those who,

while in foreign lands, were not befriended and were not exposed to the best influences.

9. The time has come when in a more statesmanlike way the leaders of Christian thought of different races which impinge upon each other should seek to promote interracial coöperation in counsel and in action. Here we have an instructive example in the results achieved in the Southern States of America within a little more than a decade by the Commission on Interracial Coöperation. The war served to inflame racial relationships between the whites and blacks of America. As a result, some of the more discerning leaders of both races in the Southern States became burdened with solicitude and initiated measures the beneficent results of which become more and more apparent day by day. Beginning in the year 1918, before the war closed, some of the best informed of the Christian leaders among the whites launched a plan. Within two years the leaders of the Negro race were led to join them, and thus was established the full Interracial Commission, composed of leading white men and women and leading men and women of the Negro race. This commission had the general oversight of the program of furthering right relations between the two races throughout the entire Southern States of America. Similar interracial commissions were then organized in each of the thirteen Southern States, each, like the general body, being composed of men and women of both races. In addition to

these bodies, interracial commissions were set up in 800 of the 1,300 counties of these thirteen States. All these groups included men and women of both races, and invariably those of real influence within their respective races were chosen. These bodies, general, state, and county, gave themselves to united study of the various aspects of the racial problem, and to taking necessary action in the direction of correcting injustices and otherwise improving conditions. It is not necessary to indicate the many practical methods which have been evolved and put into effect. The important thing to emphasize is that almost unbelievable results have already been achieved in the way of promoting better understanding, better feeling, and more fruitful action in the righting of wrongs and the averting of perils. Largely through this agency the number of lynchings was reduced from eighty-three in 1919 to ten in 1929. By common consent among observing people of both races, this work of coöperation in thought and effort constitutes the most hopeful advance ever made in the furthering of right relationships between these two races. The reports of what has been achieved have awakened such interest in other parts of the world that deputations from Europe and Africa have visited America to study at first hand this fruitful experience, which has invaluable suggestions for every part of the world where the racial problem looms large. A similar agency has now been developed in South Africa, which, under the name of the South African Institute of Race Relations, co-ordinates various local joint councils.

10. It is of fundamental importance that the Christian leaders of races especially concerned give more thought to the formation of right public opinion. In some way the collaboration of the press must be more intelligently and more largely enlisted, because the press to-day exerts enormous influence. Most unfortunately in some parts of the world that influence seems to tend more toward inflaming race relationships and strengthening race prejudice than in the opposite direction. Of coördinate importance are the cinema, or movies, and the theater. It is positively alarming to see what fires of racial prejudice are being kindled and fanned by certain films and plays which are tolerated in parts of the world and which are veritable tinder boxes. It is not only alarming, but criminal. It calls for international, as well as interracial, collaboration. I see no other way than that the Christians must increasingly take the initiative. In this connection *The Christian Century* is to be commended for its courageous, aggressive, and effective leadership. Possibly even more important than influencing the attitude of the press and those in charge of the cinema and the theater is it that there be conducted a continuous, intensive educational campaign in connection with the primary, secondary, and high schools. If those who in the most plastic years throng these institutions can be influenced aright as to

ideals, habits, and relationships, the result will doubtless be the speedy effecting of many of the other points
in this policy.

11. Christians should wage uncompromising warfare
against everything which experience shows tends to promote racial misunderstanding and strife, warfare not
only against ignorance and prejudice but also against all
unjust or unequal arrangements, laws, and practices.

12. The absolutely unique importance of the mission of Christianity with reference to the solution of the
race problem will be clearly recognized. In its aspect as a coöperative enterprise between races and not
simply a mission from one race to another, it is by
far the most extensive and influential means to insure
right racial understanding, good will, and coöperation.
Why? Because it is world-wide in its vision, program,
and ramifications. It embraces all races of mankind.
It is the most impressive example of the possibility,
practicability, and advantages of the union of all races
for common service. It has as its commanding vision
humanity as a brotherhood. This rests on the solid
Christian basis, as we have seen, of the recognition of
Jesus Christ as Lord and of men as brothers in Him.
The world mission thus believes that the principle of
brotherhood transcends all accidents of race. It recognizes and accepts the obligation to make Christ known,
loved, and obeyed among all races. It believes in the
providential mission of each race. It stands for the

fullest development and expression of each race, therefore: not for the oneness of uniformity, but for unity in
diversity. To appreciate the fullness of Christ and the
marvel of His Gospel and program we need such a
demonstration. The missionary movement the world
over is lifting the races into self-respect, true worthi-
ness, a sense of spiritual equality, and a realization of
their infinite possibilities, as well as bringing them into
friendly coöperation and uniting them in world service. Its unifying influence becomes more and more apparent day by day.

13. At a time like this it is supremely important that
in face of issues like the race problem the Christian
Church has such an organ as the International Missionary Council—to help coördinate research, thinking,
planning, and action of the constructive forces of Christendom. At its recent meeting in Jerusalem the subject
of race relations received intense attention. This body
and the various national councils related to it are in a
position to do more than possibly any other agency to
give effect to the foregoing proposals as well as to its
own comprehensive program. Particular attention is
called to the following sections of the findings adopted
at Jerusalem, where more than in any other Christian
gathering ever held were blended the various races of
mankind:

"All Christian forces, and particularly the International
Missionary Council, dedicated as they are to prepare for the

establishment among all mankind of the Kingdom of God, are bound to work with all their power to remove race prejudice and adverse conditions due to it, to preserve the rights of peoples, and to establish educational, religious, and other facilities designed to enable all alike to enjoy equality of social, political, and economic opportunity." [1]

"While we thank God for the courageous, persevering, and prophetic action taken by many communities and individuals toward achieving the will of Christ in the improvement of interracial relationships in areas where such friction is particularly acute, we confess with humiliation that we in the Christian churches are still far from realizing this principle even within our own borders.

"It is the duty of the Christian forces everywhere, and particularly of the International Missionary Council and its constituent bodies, to learn more fully the mind of Christ on the problem of interracial relations, and to press forward boldly the realization of permanent world-wide understanding." [2]

"Christians, collectively and individually, are also called, under the guidance of God and in faith in His supernatural resources, to courageous and discerning action, with a view to the ultimate victory of the will of Christ over all interracial antagonism. We would emphasize the need that each national missionary or Christian council or committee, where unchristian conditions provocative of such antagonism prevail or threaten to develop, should work toward a Christian solution." [3]

"The missionary enterprise itself, as an instrument of God for bringing into being among all races the Church of Christ, has it in its power to be the most creative force working for world-wide interracial unity. For ultimately our closest

---

[1] *The Christian Mission in the Light of Race Conflict.* The Jerusalem Meeting of the International Missionary Council, March 24–April 8, 1928, Vol. IV, p. 195 (New York: The International Missionary Council, 1928). Copyright. Used by permission.

[2] *Ibid.*, pp. 195 f.   [3] *Ibid.*, p. 200.

union with each other is our union with Him; and His commandment, 'Do unto others as ye would men should do unto you,' and 'That ye love one another even as I have loved you,' if carried into practice in all relationships, would solve the problem, and rid the world of this stupendous menace." [4]

14. Jesus Christ, and Jesus Christ only, can solve the race problem. For some reason, however, which should never fail to move us with awe, He does not accomplish this wonder work apart from human instrumentality. He seems to require the collaboration of His followers in affording and keeping open the channels through which He may communicate His superhuman impulses of wisdom, love, and power. Nevertheless, in the final analysis, it is He who accomplishes the miracle.

[4] *Ibid.*, p. 201.

World - Christian
Unity ch. V & VII.
(p. 62, 89, 99 - Chao. 2.)

Thomas

Weed 196~197

Discerning leaders all across the world, as they face the overwhelming need of the vast areas of life that we have just surveyed, see that the Christian forces, if they act separately and with no common goal or strategy, are doomed to tragic failure. Divided, they neither express the mind of Christ nor can work His will. The first essential, if mankind is to be won, if evil is to be vanquished, and if the mechanistic forces of modern life are to be subdued to God's will, is that Christians should find a world fellowship in which they can pray, plan, and labor unitedly.

Above all the new passionate emphasis on self-determination and the resultant nationalistic and racial antagonisms that we have reviewed throw upon Christians a unique responsibility for revealing in actual life the power of Christ in His Church to transcend all those differences and to create a world fellowship.

For these reasons the Meeting of the International Missionary Council at Jerusalem in the spring of 1928 was a most timely gathering. It would have been difficult, if not impossible, to bring such a representative body there at an earlier date; and one shrinks from the thought of what the world mission would have lost had the meeting been held later. It was a forward-looking assembly. More than any other convention of the Christians of modern times it listened to prophetic voices and caught the vision of the coming day. It was likewise courageous. When has a group of Christians confronted so many grave challenges? Time has already shown that the days spent by this company in fellowship, consultation, and intercession on the Mount of Olives were truly creative. Something took place there of rare propagating power, the influence of which has been world-wide and will never die. And it was a pronouncedly coöperative assemblage. One of the words or conceptions most distinctive of the Jerusalem Meeting—one which, I venture to say, will ever be associated with the occasion—was that of *sharing*.

The Jerusalem Meeting has already exerted a wider and, in some respects, a more profound influence than the World Missionary Conference which met at Edinburgh two decades ago. This intensification of power is due to the prevailing world situation. One need only contrast the conditions and trends which characterize the two periods to realize the force of this consideration. Moreover, the world missionary enterprise had reached a stage of development which made possible results at

the later period which could not have been realized two
decades ago. The very fact that there had been an
Edinburgh Conference made possible something of
greater power and outreach. There could be nothing
more dishonoring to the memorable meeting on the
heights of Edinburgh than to say it had not prepared the
way for something still more potent and promising.
This suggests another factor which in itself explains why
in such a short time the more recent meeting has exercised the wider influence. At the time of the Edinburgh
Conference there were only two national missionary
councils; at the time of the Jerusalem there were twenty-six, of which one-half were in the countries which
send missionaries and one-half in lands to which missionaries are sent. Whereas at the close of Edinburgh,
furthermore, there existed simply a temporary and, in a
sense, an unofficial Continuation Committee, at the time
of Jerusalem there existed the International Missionary
Council composed of official representatives of all the
many national councils. Thus there was a comprehensive and efficient organization through which the
ideas, program, and impulses of Jerusalem could be
authoritatively and promptly conveyed throughout
Christendom. Furthermore, the Jerusalem Meeting, unlike Edinburgh, adopted definite findings covering the
wide range of opportunity and obligation confronting
the world mission. This enabled the delegates to go
forth from the Mount of Olives prepared to bring to

bear upon their problems immediately and unitedly the new light and power which they had received. But the outstanding reason explaining the unique and wonderful influence of Jerusalem is the dynamic fact emphasized above—that the Christian leaders there assembled from all parts of the world came to realize as never before that the world mission is preëminently a sharing enterprise. Jerusalem is not to be thought of simply as a landmark, but rather as a new creation. Those who were present were conscious that they were in the midst of one of the great creative hours of the world mission and expansion of Christianity.

The great change which has taken place in the world in the past two decades may best be illustrated if the Edinburgh and Jerusalem meetings are contrasted in one very important respect. At Edinburgh the number of nationals representing the so-called mission lands was almost negligible. In all there were less than a score among the 1,200 regular delegates and over 2,000 unofficial visitors. These were there not by design of the organizing committee, or of the indigenous churches. On the other hand, at Jerusalem fully one-third of the delegates from the fifty-one countries represented came from the rising churches of Asia, Africa, Latin America, and the island world. The aim was to have approximately equal numbers from these churches and from those of Europe, North America, and Australasia, and this was virtually the case, if we do not count the delegates who were coöpted as experts to supply information on certain problems. Thus the Jerusalem Meeting was the first world Christian conference ever held in which the representatives of the older churches, which have sent forth the missionaries, and of the younger churches, which have been founded by the missionaries, met on substantially a parity as to numbers, and, even more important, on an equality as to strength, status, leadership, contribution of ideas and experience, and influence in shaping program and policy. This basic fact made possible something truly wonderful and highly significant. An atmosphere was generated in which, to use words spoken by Bishop Gore years ago, we came "to loathe to differ and to determine to understand." It means much to have an atmosphere in which Christians strongly dislike to differ, but it is a more wonderful and hopeful thing to find ourselves in an atmosphere in which we highly resolve to understand each other. This makes possible the discovery of emancipating truth. As better understanding was created at Jerusalem between those of the older and the younger churches, their confidence in each other deepened. Then Christian love could more fully manifest itself. Before long we began to realize, more fully and vividly than ever before, that we are indispensable to each other. As the days of fellowship in thought and prayer unfolded we became conscious of our deep spiritual solidarity. Thereafter, it became easy to project large and heroic plans together,

and to contemplate ever-increasing coöperative effort.
I repeat, this was the first time in the history of the
world mission when on a world scale the two great
streams, the older and the younger churches, have been
so blended. The very use of the nomenclature "older"
and "younger" churches is in itself very significant.
The old phraseology could no longer adequately express
the realities. Jerusalem did more than all other factors
to bring in the day in which the missionary enterprise
will be regarded as a sharing enterprise on the part of
both older and younger churches. Henceforth all countries where Christian churches exist will be regarded as
sending countries; that is, will be considered as lands
from which missionaries should go. All such should
be regarded also as receiving countries. All countries
where Christ has His witnesses should consider themselves as home-base countries as in the days of the early
Christian Church.

With this conception in mind of the world mission
as a sharing enterprise let us first consider what both
the older and the younger churches should share with
each other. In other words, what are some of the things
which they should have in common?

Without doubt younger and older churches alike
should unite in a quest for truth, should join to discover
more and more of the truth which enlightens, emanci-
pates, enlarges, enriches, vitalizes, energizes. This is
not all revealed through any one nation, race, or com-

munion. Christ requires all groups through whom to manifest His fullness. How true it is, as each successive generation demonstrates, that there is ever new truth to break out through God's Word and through His children. While truth may be one, it is constantly manifesting itself through new forms, facets, illustrations, experiences, glories. In the wide field of original research, with reference to problems involved in making Christ known, and in applying His principles to all human relationships, it is highly desirable that the Christians of the churches of the East and the West, the North and the South, collaborate and share with one another their insight, knowledge, and experience.

The leaders and members of the older and the younger churches should share with each other their visions. In every age and in every land and in every communion there are some men and women who have visions of the expanding Kingdom which are priceless and should be shared. It is true now as in ancient times that "where there is no vision the people perish." May not the reason why the work of the churches in some fields stagnates lie right here, that some who have spent time on the mountains and have received a commanding vision have not shared it, or, at best, have imparted it only to those of their own racial or denominational group? Rufus Jones not only became alarmed as he saw the imminent dangers to the spiritual life of the world from the mighty oncoming tide of secularism but he also caught a vision of Christ's adequacy to resist and overcome. He could give himself no rest without sharing his vision and conviction. So during these past few years in his burning addresses in America, in Europe, and in Asia and in many an article, notably in his paper on *Secular Civilization and the Christian Task* prepared for the Jerusalem Meeting, his God-implanted vision has been communicated to all churches and has come to countless Christians with contagious power.

This experience suggests that not only visions and messages but also creative personalities themselves should be shared. Dr. E. Stanley Jones finds in India, the land with which he has so completely identified himself and which he serves with such passionate devotion, needs which might absorb all his years and power, and no one can question his wisdom in making that his permanent base and the major object of his service. But likewise one cannot doubt the divine leading which has sent him for limited periods to Anglo-Saxon America, to Latin America, to Europe, and other parts of the world to share his experience of Christ. The reflex influence of such unselfish services is always highly multiplying. This has been illustrated again and again by the visits of Dr. Kagawa to China and America.

There should also be far more sharing of dynamic spiritual literature. All over the world and in various languages there are appearing books and magazine articles which convey truth calculated to contribute powerfully to the building up of faith and character and to the widening and deepening of the work of organized Christianity. More comprehensive plans must be evolved to insure the proper translation and more general introduction or circulation of such works. Issues which but a few years ago were regarded as solely of national or denominational significance are now coming to be recognized as of world-wide concern. This is preeminently true of the great world religion, Christianity. The writings on the social gospel by Kagawa of Japan, the spiritual experiences of Sadhu Sundar Singh, *My Life in Christ* by Father John of the Russian Orthodox Church, *The Life of Gairdner of Cairo* by Miss Constance Padwick, the life of Aggrey of Africa by Edwin W. Smith, Miss Evelyn Underhill's writings on prayer and mysticism, the devotional thoughts of Navarro Monzó of South America, Rauschenbusch's *Prayers of the Social Awakening*, Otto's *The Idea of the Holy*, and Barth's *Word of God and Word of Man*—to mention at random only a few relatively recent works—are books by Christians of quite different religious background, but all have a living message for the Christians of various lands and churches.

The time has come when more than in the past Christian leaders need to unite in determining the strategy for the Christian forces. We imperatively require what the French in the World War called grand strategy. By this was meant the strategy that took in all fronts.

Christianity has world problems. Christianity the world over has certain common enemies and perils. Christianity has ever had, given by her Founder, a common Gospel. Increasingly the world mission is arriving at a common program. To overcome the powers that oppose she must develop and employ a united strategy. It is vain otherwise to think of waging victorious warfare against the opium evil, the white slave traffic, forced labor, atheistic destructive communism, race prejudice and strife, or secularism. In other words, Christians on every continent who influence the thought and action must more and more come to see eye to eye as to objectives and as to disposition and use of forces.

There is still much pioneering work to do in the spread of the Christian religion. There are great areas in Central Asia, in many parts of Africa, in some sections of Latin America which are still completely unoccupied—that is, without missionaries. Heretofore the task of entering such fields has been left almost entirely with the older churches of Europe, North America, and Australasia. Has not the time come when the younger churches of Asia, Africa, and Latin America should share with them this responsibility? It is a serious fact that of the list of fields submitted at the Edinburgh Conference twenty years ago as unoccupied relatively few have since been entered. If the Chinese and Indian workers were to unite with Europeans and Americans, might it not facilitate greatly the spread of the Gospel in inner Asia? And if earnest Christians among the Red Indians of the United States and Canada should join forces with those of Anglo-Saxon and Latin countries, would it not prove to be a great advantage in reaching the millions of unevangelized Indians of Central and South America? There is a great work also waiting among the Chinese, Japanese, and Indian peoples in Malaya and in the islands of the Pacific which can best be done by representatives of the churches of China, Japan, and India.

At a time like this the members of both older and younger churches may well give heed to the injunction of the great missionary apostle, "Bear ye one another's burdens, and so fulfill the law of Christ." All churches which are to-day true to the implications of Christ's commands and teachings find themselves heavy laden. They need one another's support. Wherever this mutual burden-bearing is in evidence it constitutes a convincing apologetic of the reality and wonder-working power of Christ's law. How little after all, however, do the churches on different sides of the oceans enter into fellowship with one another in lifting impossible loads and meeting baffling difficulties and at times persecution and suffering. Here lie great possibilities of sharing to be explored.

In this matter of mutual sharing a good illustration to keep in mind is that of the cantilever bridge. In its construction the two arms are built or projected toward

each other simultaneously and, if true to pattern, ultimately meet, fit perfectly, and constitute a complete
unity. This is the secret of the bridge's stability and
strength. Thus perfected it makes possible constant
commerce backward and forward between the two sides
and between the great regions that lie beyond on either
side. It is believed that the process of mutual sharing
between the older and the younger churches which has
been so expanded and accelerated by the understandings
entered into and the unity achieved at Jerusalem will, as
it is faithfully carried forward, greatly facilitate world-
wide, united fellowship, planning, and action.

In addition to the part which the older churches share
in common or mutually with the younger churches, there
are some things which the older churches only have to
contribute to the younger churches. Their great contribution of this kind is that of placing at the disposal
of the rising indigenous churches of Asia, Africa, and
Latin America the lessons from their experiences
throughout the centuries. Great and irreparable would
be the loss which the younger churches would suffer from
being cut off from this experience. It would involve
missing the lessons of historical Christianity, for it is
impossible to mention a single century in the life of the
Christian Church which does not have invaluable lessons to teach new churches. Some of these are lessons
of example to follow, others of dangers or courses to
avoid. It would also be unwise to miss the lessons

which come from the thorough study of creedal Christianity. This does not imply that creeds should be taken over bodily or in part. It does mean that the great mental and spiritual struggles which have attended the working out, defense, revision, and propagation of the great creeds of Christendom, as well as some of those that are more obscure, abound in teaching now by incitement, now by warning, which will be of incalculable value to those who in the fields of the Orient, Africa, and elsewhere are charged with the responsibility of developing new churches and training their leaders. Then there are lessons to be drawn from the experience of Christianity the world over—that is, universal Christianity. In my life of world-wide travel, of repeated and prolonged visits to many lands, I have had opportunity to study at first hand the life, the working, and the influence of most of the so-called older churches as well as of those called younger. In the light of these contacts and studies, I should find it difficult to mention any country in which these older churches have existed or still exist, the story of which the leaders of Christianity in new fields may ignore. In some of the most unlikely fields I have learned some of the most significant facts and useful lessons. Think also of mystical Christianity, for example, as illustrated by the Russian Orthodox Church or by the Society of Friends. When I consider how my own life has been enriched by these communions I crave similar contacts for the Christians of other continents than those where these communions had their rise. Moreover, the phrases "applied Christianity" and "vital or transforming Christianity" at once suggest what a tremendous loss any Christian church or Christian leader would suffer who consciously or unconsciously might be cut off from the groups of Christians in the older churches as well as in the younger who are thus intimately associated with the religion of Christ in action. In the period right before us more than at any time in the past, possibly more than at any time in the future, the leaders of the younger churches need such exposure as is here emphasized. This fact is due to conditions and forces outside these churches and also to the problems within the churches themselves.

How can the older churches share the lessons of the experience of their past and present? The answer to this question can best be worked out in consultation with the leaders of the younger churches. In the light of many such conversations and discussions, I will mention some of the ways and means.

More missionaries will have to be sent. A misconception exists in some quarters as to whether more are needed. In other places it is thought that while more may be needed, they are not wanted. The uncertainty on these points has led to several recent extensive inquiries. The result in all these instances has been to make it clear beyond question that in the aggregate a large number of well-qualified missionaries are not only greatly needed but wanted by the Christian nationals of the countries concerned. It has been strongly emphasized, however, that the new missionaries must average higher in qualifications and equipment than has generally obtained in the past, and that is saying a great deal. Again it has been stressed that in the period right before us workers with more highly specialized training will be required. This demand is due to the more advanced stage in education of the peoples to be served. The growth of the spirit of nationalism has a vital bearing on the subject. Another consideration is the marked development of independence and autonomy of the churches themselves, and also the fact that they have arrived at a stage calling for more specialization in the church program and work. The need to share the experience of the Church of other centuries and countries should affect policy and practice both in choosing and in training candidates for missionary service.

Besides regular missionaries chosen with reference to life service or to prolonged periods of service, it is desirable to send out for short periods authorities or experts on certain subjects. Good illustrations are the contributions made in the recent past in the realm of apologetics by Canon Streeter, of Oxford, Professor Rufus Jones, of Haverford, Principal Cairns, of Aberdeen—while visiting the Orient; the work in the interest of religious education in Latin America accomplished by Dr. W. C. Barclay and in China by Dr. J. L. Corley, and more recently the guidance on rural problems afforded by Dr. Butterfield on his extended visits to South Africa, India, and the Far East; and the work in India of the Higher Educational Commission, composed of leading educationalists of Great Britain and America, having as their chairman Dr. A. D. Lindsay, the Master of Balliol. Each year hundreds of distinguished university professors who are in a position to speak with authority or give counsel on subjects of vital importance to the Christian movement take a sabbatical year. If the matter is planned and taken up with them well in advance, not a few of those whose services are most needed could doubtless be obtained for all or a large part of the year. Some of them might be used in visiting a number of centers; others might make their best contribution if attached to some one institution. In certain instances one denomination might finance and direct the work of the visitors; in others it might better be conducted under interdenominational auspices. The various national Christian councils are often in the best position to take charge of such arrangements.

The older churches should always be ready to respond to appeals for the help of their best-equipped men in times of nation-wide movements of evangelism such as are now in progress in Japan and China. The pressing of the advantage which such movements of the Spirit of God afford is a matter of supreme concern to the entire Church of Christ. No one is too busy or too important to be called upon to consider such appeals.

For many a year the older churches and their constituencies will be called upon to coöperate financially in the programs of the younger churches. They are in lands well able to render such assistance and without doubt the help will be needed. To extend this needed coöperation in ways which will permanently help and not weaken the rising churches constitutes one of the questions calling for more scientific study than it has yet received. By scientific study is meant study which is impartial, thorough, and accurate and which takes account of all the facts and factors. It is admitted that many mistakes have been made in the past. A vast amount of experience has been accumulated and is now becoming increasingly available. A number of careful studies have been made by individuals and groups, and some by whole denominations or other agencies. Happily the lessons are being more and more brought to bear and with gratifying results. There is need of coordinating the extensive and varied knowledge and experience, and steps are being taken to this end by the International Missionary Council and other bodies. Missionary board administrators and leaders of the younger churches are collaborating much more closely in giving effect to the policy of self-support. Apart from the support of the local churches themselves, there will be needed, and under proper conditions there can be wisely given, large sums to support such work as the missionaries themselves do, also toward many forms of institutional work, toward permanent equipment, toward introducing certain forms of specialization, and, now and then, toward fostering significant forward movements.

A heavy obligation rests upon the older churches to strengthen the hands of the younger churches by doing all in their power to befriend and to serve the nationals who come to sojourn for longer or shorter periods in the countries of Europe and North America for study, business, government service, travel, or other purposes. Those who come as Christians should be brought into vital relation to the churches and to Christian homes. Those who are not Christians should be exposed to the best side of the life of the country and be helped in establishing friendly ties with Christian people. Services of the utmost value have been rendered by such agencies as the Committee on Promoting Friendly Relations among Foreign Students and the student Christian movements in general. Individual families, individual local churches, and other specially organized local groups have shown what is possible in the way of real Christian hospitality; but it is feared that only a small fraction of those who come within the gates of foreign lands are thus befriended. The whole matter should receive much more masterly attention. It may be questioned whether there is any one thing which the older churches can do, within the field of sharing, which will be more helpful to the younger churches than that of performing the highest offices of friendship to these strangers in strange lands.

The next question is, What have the younger churches to share with the older churches in addition to what the older and the younger churches share in common?

First of all, they often afford present-day illustrations of early Christianity. Every student of the apostolic age who has also been a discerning traveler in lands to which Christianity has recently come remarks on how often the latter conditions and developments remind him of those which obtained in the days of the primitive Church. This explains why many a leader in the older churches comes back from a visit to the mission field so greatly refreshed and strengthened in faith. The time the leaders and other Christians in the so-called non-Christian countries spend with Christian travelers from Europe and America exposing them to the life and work of their churches will be time well spent.

Much more than is usually realized, the Christians of Asia, Africa, and Latin America have a vital spiritual experience to share with those of the West. All those who come into close contact with Chinese Christian visitors to the West, such as the eminent Christian educator, Chang Po-ling, and the truly great Chinese prophet, Dr. C. Y. Cheng, can bear grateful testimony to this

fact'. Sadhu Sundar Singh while in Europe made a
profound impression wherever he went. A friend of
mine from Sweden told me that his coming was nearer
having Christ visit her home than had been that of any
other guest she had ever welcomed. Regarding his influence I quote also the testimony of Sir Francis Younghusband in his book, *Dawn in India:*

"Another Indian who has gained a European reputation
is the Christian mystic, Sundar Singh. . . . His Christianity impressed even Christian Europe. In every European
country he was received with honor; crowded audiences listened to his addresses; biographies of him have been written
in English, German, French, and Swedish; and the distinguished theologian, Friedrich Heiler, has written a combined
biography and critical appreciation of his message, which has
passed through four German editions and been translated into
English.

". . . . The significance of his life lies in this, that it gives
us an indication as to how Christianity can best be presented
to India, and perhaps Europe too. The Sadhu from his youth
had caught the true inward spirit of Christ. He had been
seeking God and seeking true spiritual peace with his whole
heart. And the vision or appearance of Jesus to him as a
young man had actually given him that peace. And quite
simply he had borne witness all over the world to the joy and
peace which he had found. The spirit of Christ had entered
deeply into him and filled his whole being. And it was thoroughly congenial to his Indian soul. He could well understand it. But he was right when he followed his own deep-felt
conviction and decided to go forth, not as a Europeanized
Indian, but in the true Indian rôle of a Sadhu. The Christian
message had to be given to India in an Indian way. He could
thus testify in a way that Indians could understand—and in
a way that European Christians, too, could understand." [1]

[1] Sir Francis Younghusband, *Dawn in India*, pp. 301, 311 f. (London:
John Murray, 1930). Copyright.

Possibly no better indication could be given that the leaders and members of the older churches do look with sincerity and eager expectancy to the Christians of the East for spiritual help than the fact that the Standing Committee of the Missionary Societies of Great Britain and Ireland have invited the National Christian Council of India, Burma, and Ceylon to send a religious mission to share with British Christians the religious treasures of the Indian Church.

May it not be that the churches of the West may also learn lessons from the devotional practices of their fellow Christians in the Orient? Missionaries in India, for example, after studying the plan known as the Ashram are increasingly realizing its spiritual helpfulness. The one established by Father Winslow at Poona is recognized as a fountain of spiritual vitality. Dr. E. Stanley Jones after much prayer and thought has also recently opened another. The following outline of his purpose and plan is suggestive:

"The purpose and spirit of the . . . Ashram might be stated as follows:

"To yoke the Christian spirit and the Indian spirit in the service of Christ and India.

"To endeavor to produce a type of Christianity more in touch with the soul of India and more aflame with the love of Christ.

"In order to fulfill the above aims we propose to have a group of specially invited Indians and Europeans who shall, in group meditation and devotion and study, endeavor to think through the problems of the relationship of our Gospel to the other faiths of the world and especially of India, and of the relationship of our lives and work to the future of India. In addition to this group of the specially invited we will welcome those who care to join us from time to time.

"This group will live in Indian style, eat Indian food, and wear Indian dress. As we hope to have Hindus join us the food will be vegetarian. This group will share the same bungalow and outcottage. No distinctions will be made. We hope to break down all barriers.

"As one of the chief marks of the Indian spirit is simplicity this group will live in simplicity, have few or no servants, work with their hands in the bungalow and in the surrounding gardens, and serve each other generally.

"We shall endeavor to learn sympathetically the languages, culture, and religions of India in order to have a more sympathetic approach to the people. At the same time we shall endeavor to hold a passionate devotion to the mind and purpose and person of Christ. We hope to make the Indian spirit creative in art, in music, and in Christian thinking.

". . . We will endeavor . . . to create new centers of understanding of India and a passionate devotion to Jesus Christ in various parts of the country. . . .

"The Ashram will be Christian but will know nothing of denominational lines. In our worship we shall endeavor to take that which will best express the Christian spirit. At the same time we hope the worship will express the finest of the Indian spirit. We trust that prayer will be the very breath of the Ashram." [2]

The younger churches can help the older churches to meet certain attacks and criticisms regarding the missionary movement. At times Oriental students studying in the universities of Europe and America assert that no more missionaries from the West are needed or wanted in their countries. By far the best way to meet this un-

[2] E. Stanley Jones, in *The Indian Social Reformer*, Vol. XL, January 11, 1930, pp. 310 f. (Bombay, India).

settling charge is for an able Christian national to visit
certain universities and student conferences, as did T. Z.
Koo and K. T. Paul, and in an authoritative and completely convincing way give the actual facts. Again,
American or British business men come back from the
Orient and assert that Christian missions are doing more
harm than good, and that the people of these countries
do not want them. Here also the presence of a leading
Japanese Christian layman, like Dr. Nitobé, or a Chinese Christian merchant, like the representative of the
Shanghai Commercial Press, speaking before chambers
of commerce is able, as is no returned missionary, to set
matters in their true light. Much more sharing of
knowledge, conviction, and influence is going to be
needed in years to come.

The time has come when Oriental and Latin American
evangelists, apologists, and personal witnesses as to the
power and sufficiency of Christ can come with arresting
and convicting power before large audiences and open
forums. This is largely an unworked lead, but it is
one to which increasing attention must be given. When
it was learned a few months ago that Dr. Kagawa of
Japan was contemplating a short visit to North America
the committee in charge of his program were deluged
with invitations from all kinds of organizations, religious and secular. This experience suggests one of the
ways in which the younger churches are at the present
time doing most to help the churches of the West, and

that is by quickening and expanding their faith. In no other way can this be more surely and effectively done than by letting first-hand participants, or witnesses, like Bishop Azariah, describe that wonder work of God, the mass movement of India, or, like Navarro Monzó, tell of the remarkable spiritual movement among the intelligentsia of Latin America, or, like C. Y. Cheng, describe the launching of the Five-Year Movement among the churches of China in the face of the greatest combination of obstacles and discouragements which the Christians of any country in these days are called upon to face. Such testimonies and the mighty demonstrations to which they bear witness put to shame the unworthy plans and little faith of the churches of the West.

Again, the younger churches can greatly help the older churches by their multiplying examples of Christian unity. On almost every field in the non-Christian world—in the Far East, in the Near East, in Eastern Asia, and in Latin America—marked progress is being made to unite the Christian forces. One of the most notable examples is that of the United Church of South India, which gives promise of bringing to full fruition the plan on which they have been working for many years. Another is the Church of Christ in China, in which already some fourteen denominations, including one-third of the Protestant Christians of China, have united.

What is the secret of realizing more fully the conception of the world mission of Christianity as a sharing enterprise? In answer, it is of basic importance that both older and younger churches strive unitedly to develop and maintain their churches as truly indigenous and living churches.

Missionaries were formerly regarded and spoken of in the younger churches as leaders, teachers, masters. Increasingly they will regard themselves as coöperators, colleagues, partners, helpers. As Paul expressed it, "not that we have lordship over your faith, but are helpers of your joy." This principle of devolution is so difficult of achievement, yet so vitally essential, if Christianity is to respond to the world need, that the following chapter is devoted to it.

THERE IS NEED TO-DAY OF A greater awareness of certain present-day tendencies in the rising indigenous churches throughout the world, and of drawing certain lessons from the vast and rich experience of these churches with the clear end in view of fostering their larger initiative, increased sense of responsibility, and strengthened leadership. There is general agreement that the raising up of indigenous churches is our goal. Thousands of the finest missionaries and indigenous church leaders have poured out their lives working toward the realization of this objective. Moreover, this has been a central object in their prayers, and these prayers have been answered to a far greater degree than is generally realized. Without doubt there are rising in all parts of the mission field genuine indigenous churches. Let me call attention to some developments and tendencies which will help us to recognize the characteristics of such churches.

Indigenous churches are those in which the nationals find themselves at home, and that impress even their non-Christian friends as natural, homelike, and belonging to the country. The churches which seem to be rooting themselves most deeply in the soil are also those which do not trample on long-established and much-valued good customs and ideals. The location of the church building has a suggestion as to whether it is becoming indigenous. In some fields these churches are located on the missionary compound—that is, the enclosure where the homes of the foreign leaders are located. If a church is truly indigenous, the church edifice is planted right in the heart of the people, wherever they are. The matter of church architecture is also more than a detail from the point of view of the nationals. And yet how many churches remind one more of churches in Britain, Germany, or America than of truly Asiatic and African traditions. Some have perfectly impossible architecture from the point of view of the climate. What a strange impression it must make upon the national, in contrast with an architecture adapted to what means most to him in point of comfort, homelikeness, and the spirit of worship. The arrangement inside the church building is important. Recently I was in a church in one of the fields of the Far East where a foreign missionary had insisted on having chairs, although in every other kind of meeting in that section the people preferred to sit on mats on the floor. Then in the matter of organization, what strange impressions people must get as they study this aspect of

the life of indigenous churches.   In China one might
well wonder whether there had not been another Tower
of Babel, for in some provinces you would find reproduced the results in organization of century-long ecclesiastical controversies of Europe and America.   As a rule
these involve questions not vital to making Christ known,
loved, and obeyed.   It will be generally recognized that
there are certain lessons in polity and organization
which are of permanent value.   As a rule discerning
church leaders in Asia and Africa are ready to accept
as a guiding principle whatever has its anchorage in the
teachings of Christ and the Apostles.   They are not convinced that they ought to reproduce everything which
has happened in the life of the churches in other countries in the intervening centuries.

In the matter of forms of church worship, the indigenous church leaders are doing not a little thinking.
They are wondering why they should not be given larger
freedom of expression.   They value highly the experience of the churches of the West, but the churches of
the West were permitted to evolve their own ways of
worshiping God together.   They not only crave this same
freedom, but they desire encouragement to this end.

Moreover, in many indigenous churches, self-support
is recognized as a fundamental characteristic.   Upon
the whole, there is ground for encouragement.   In some
fields where we might have least expected it they have
achieved a large measure of self-support.   In some coun-

tries they are not only supporting their own local parish churches, but are also helping to support the educational work, the medical work, and other Christian institutions. All over the non-Christian world there are springing up native missionary societies which are supporting missionaries of their own. This sign of the anchoring of the church in the life of the people is indeed reassuring. Of course, there is always room for improvement. That is true in the West as well as in the East. It is true in rich countries as well as in impoverished countries. The Christians on some mission fields where economic conditions are most difficult are putting to shame those who are most favorably circumstanced financially.

Self-government is another characteristic of a genuine indigenous church. We cannot call a church truly indigenous if it is controlled from outside its own nationality. This is where there have been, and still are, the most misunderstandings and the largest lack of trust on both sides. What do we mean in our prayers when we ask God to raise up an indigenous church? Do we mean a church that foreigners will always keep their hands on and guide; or do we mean a church which will some day take the reins and work out its own destiny? Happily in an increasing number of churches the missionaries have put themselves under the nationals.

A truly indigenous church is also self-propagating. In fact, this whole problem is one of vitality more than one of autonomy. If there is life, it will reproduce itself. This is surely what Christ had in mind when he gave the parable of the branches and the vine. If Christians anywhere are grafted into the living Christ, there is life there. The thoughtful student of the subject will come to the conclusion that Christ has communicated Himself to churches all over the non-Christian world.

We may well ponder the definition agreed upon by the Jerusalem Council Meeting in which these churches took an unprecedented part.

"A church, deeply rooted in God through Jesus Christ, an integral part of the Church Universal, may be said to be living and indigenous:

"1. When its interpretation of Christ and its expression in worship and service, in customs and in art and architecture incorporate the worthy characteristics of the people, while conserving at the same time the heritage of the Church in all lands and in all ages.

"2. When through it the spirit of Jesus Christ influences all phases of life, bringing to His service all the potentialities of both men and women.

"3. When it actively shares its life with the nation in which it finds itself.

"4. When it is alert to the problems of the times and, as a spiritual force in the community, courageously and sympathetically makes its contribution to their solution.

"5. When it is kindled with the missionary ardor and the pioneering spirit." [1]

The older churches should, as a major point in their

[1] *The Relation Between the Younger and the Older Churches.* The Jerusalem Meeting of the International Missionary Council, March 24– April 8, 1928, Vol. III, pp. 165 f. (New York: The International Missionary Council, 1928). Copyright. Used by permission.

policy, further in every way in their power the process
of devolution. By this is meant placing increasingly,
and as soon as possible, in the hands of the indigenous
church the power of initiative, full responsibility, and
final decision. This is absolutely necessary if the serious
handicap of being regarded as foreign is to be removed,
also if the church is to be saved from the weakness of
paternalism. It is essential to insure real self-direction,
self-support, and self-propagation. If the church is not
to fail or die, it must become indigenous. To this end,
there must be more on the part of the older church
than having devolution as a guiding principle. It must
have this as a clearly defined goal, and also fix
specific stages and periods within which definite functions and powers are to be handed over. The carrying out of the policy is attended with grave difficulties.
It involves risks. Mistakes will be made. Even so,
there is no other way. There must be great acts of
trust. In this way and in no other have vital churches
ever been developed.

There should be constant, grateful recognition that
the desired growth of independence, power of initiative,
acceptance of responsibility, and exercise of the power
of decision are in line with the working of God's unfailing laws. Among these laws are those of sowing and
reaping, of Christlike living, of intercession, and of
sacrifice. Therefore, when we know that these laws
have been made operative, that these powers have been

given right of way, then we have the right to expect the
evolution of autonomous, indigenous, living churches.

What are some of the lessons which we should lay
most to heart from these rising indigenous churches?

One is that we should avoid Westernizing them. If
we do not deliberately avoid it, the danger is that we
shall be committing this fault unconsciously.

Another lesson is that we should regard it as abnormal to have the leaders of these churches under the
control or direction of representatives of the churches
of the West. It certainly should not be regarded as the
permanent normal arrangement.

A third very important lesson is that the Christian
leaders all over the world need to use their imagination
a great deal more than they do. It is a splendid thing
to use the memory, to carry forward the invaluable lessons of experience and of what God has done through
the centuries. He intends to teach through all these
experiences. A principal subject of study in these days
by the native churches should be the study of church
history. This is one of my strongest convictions. I believe the Living Christ has been teaching through every
generation lessons absolutely invaluable. None of them
should be lost. It will contribute to the strength of any
rising church to draw on those lessons. But it does not
nullify this point to insist on the exercise also of imagination. That is only another way of saying that we
should try to put ourselves at the point of view of these

rising churches, that we should try to understand them, that we should try to get into their minds, and, above all, that we should try to understand their hearts. That is difficult, but it is very Christlike. In other words, we of Europe and America decrease; they of Asia and Africa increase. We have prayed that there might rise up churches that will go on, churches that will not die out, churches that will spread to other lands. This is one of the great apologetics in our faith—the belief that the Living Christ has so communicated Himself to Christians of our day that, if Christianity were to die out in America and Europe, which God forbid, it exists in such vitality in Japan, Korea, China, Africa, and the islands of the Pacific that it would ultimately come back to us.

The next important point to emphasize is that if indigenous churches are to be preserved in purity and power, they must be kept strongly evangelistic and aggressively missionary. When I visited parts of Northern Africa, I was solemnized by the reminder that once over those lands there were hundreds of churches with pure doctrine, which since have perished. Why? Because they ceased to be aggressively evangelistic and missionary. A sight even sadder was that of churches still existing in the Levant which have no propagating power. Even in Europe and America there are churches with the longest and truest of creeds which, nevertheless, are not communicating vitality to others.

What is the secret of maintaining such evangelistic

spirit and propagating power? Usually the springs are to be found in secret places, perchance in little bands for prayer. I question whether there has ever been a thoroughly evangelistic church some leaders and members of which were not in secret on their knees. Another method which is spreading is that of retreats. This means is coming more and more into use among Oriental and African churches, and it seems to fit in well with their disposition and practice. One of the main criticisms I heard in China with reference to the churches was from Dr. C. Y. Cheng, the Chinese Christian leader, who presided over the last National Christian Conference in China. He said: "The principal contribution of the West to us has been activity. When we think of Western Christianity we think of a great deal of activity. What we want is more quiet." They seem to respond to this idea of retreats—that is, dropping all thought about their work and getting away from the crowd to wait unhurriedly and unitedly upon God and to yield to His sway. Must not our Lord have had this in mind when He said, "Tarry ye in the city, until ye be clothed with power from on high"? When they left that room nothing in the Roman Empire could stop them. The fires were kindled all over that inhospitable field, and influences were set in motion that made possible the rising churches of Europe—that is, the indigenous churches of Europe. Are the indigenous churches of Asia and Africa to be produced in a different way?

These churches need God-sent evangelists. People try to secure evangelists by all kinds of methods, but the evangelists who have this vital power are God-sent, like the Old Testament prophets. If in place of certain conferences church leaders and members were to give themselves in prayer, might not God thrust forth more evangelists? One explanation of vitally evangelistic churches is the fact that the pastors preach sermons in which they summon their members to wield the sickle for sheaves unto life eternal.

Moreover, in such churches personal workers' bands are one of the most fruitful methods. This is a Christlike method. It is applicable to every nation and race. Just now its use should be greatly expanded in all indigenous churches. Besides the individual work, and the work by groups, some of these churches have had the vision and courage to undertake nation-wide evangelistic campaigns. The most notable examples of this are those afforded by the churches in Japan.

There is need of strengthening greatly the native arm of the service throughout the non-Christian fields of the world. The idea of evangelizing the world apart from the raising up of a large number of highly qualified indigenous workers is, at the best, a vision not likely to be realized.

The value and importance of raising up an adequate indigenous force would seem to be evident. As a matter of economy and business sense it is desirable, because native agents can live and work in their own country at comparatively little expense. The nationals are already acclimatized, furthermore, and can work at all seasons and without furloughs. They are in intimate association with their own people: they travel together, eat together, live together. Naturally, they have a more fluent command of the vocabulary and the habitual trains of thought, the currents of feeling, and the springs of action. They understand the national character, and, other things being equal, are the best judges of the motives and sincerity of those among whom they work. They know the temptations, doubts, and soul-struggles of those with whom they are so closely associated. They have probably fought over the same battleground. They know the heart life of their fellows, and their fellows know that they know it. They are of the same blood. They will always have larger and more influential access to their own people. It took a German to lead the German Reformation. Wyclif in England and John Knox in Scotland are further illustrations of the same principle. Americans have always most deeply moved their continent. Asiatics, Africans, and Pacific islanders have ever come with greatest power to their own. And so it will ever be—the sons and daughters of the soil will leave the deepest mark on their own people and generation.

It would seem to be the Providential method. It is also the method which great missionaries have specially emphasized.   Alexander Duff, that great missionary statesman, said that "when the set time arrives the real reformers of Hindustan will be qualified Hindus."   Joseph Neesima, after years of Christian work in Japan, said that "the best possible method to evangelize her people is to raise up a native agency."   Mackay, of Uganda, who was a wiser missionary than his years and whose wisdom becomes more and more apparent as the missionary problem is grappled with in Africa, said that "the agency by which, and probably by which alone, we can Christianize Africa is the African himself.   But," he added, "he must first be trained for that work, and trained, too, by the European in Africa."   Dr. Nevius, who was conceded to be one of the ablest missionaries of China, said that "the millions of China must be brought to Christ by Chinese."   Dr. Griffith John, the great Nestor of Chinese missionaries, wrote me many years ago from the heart of China that the wonderful ingathering in Fukien, Hupeh, Hunan, and Manchuria was attributable mainly, under God, to the efficiency, the earnestness, and the assiduity of the Chinese workers.   Dr. Goodrich wrote me about the same time from North China that, "whether we view this question politically, economically, historically, or sociologically, the only sound method of evangelizing a great nation is that of raising up and using the native agency."

There are difficulties in the way of securing and using the desired workers.   There is, for example, the contempt in which religious workers are held in the East. This is unlike what we find in Australia, Canada, America, and Great Britain, where the ministry has dignity and prestige as a result of its honorable position and influence through centuries. All through Asia today, largely as a result of the corrupt lives of the Buddhist and other priests, religious callings are looked down upon, if not despised. Unwillingness to incur the reproach which so often attaches to the national who is related to the foreigner is another difficulty which keeps many from entering upon Christian service in these countries. They do not like to be called foreign hirelings, as a Japanese expressed it to me; or, as a group of Chinese put it, they do not want to be twitted with eating the foreigner's rice. Then there is the question of status, which seems to stand in the way of some in India and in other lands—that is, the national workers feel that they are entitled to more power, liberty, and responsibility than they have; that they should receive larger recognition; that more confidence should be shown in them by the missionaries. It is admitted that in not a few instances they have good reasons for this opinion. But in others, doubtless, their attitude is due to a misconception of the motives and spirit of the missionaries. Nevertheless, this is a very real difficulty, and it is not easy to overcome.

The opposition of parents and relatives is a very real hindrance. In lands where the Confucian ethics dominate, or where the system of caste exists, it is exceedingly difficult, far more than in the West, for young men to stand out against the expressed desire of parents, relatives, and friends. The attractions presented by commercial pursuits, by government service, and by other so-called secular walks of life, is a reason, if not the principal reason, why it is so difficult to-day to get a sufficient number of strong students to devote themselves to Christian work. The salaries paid in the secular callings range all the way from a little larger to thirty or more times larger than can be paid in Christian service. When one of my friends visited the Doshisha Theological Seminary in Japan a few years ago, he found there eighty theological students. Later, the number fell to less than a score. I was told by the professors that the chief cause of this decline in the number of ministerial candidates lay in the great inducements to money-making in connection with the commercial development of Japan. This is a real difficulty, and we should have sympathy with those subjected to such pressure, remembering that they have not, as a rule, like students in Europe and America, Christian heredity, Christian environment, and the dominance of Christian ideals to hold them to higher tasks.

A lack of spirituality should not be omitted among the causes making it difficult to get a sufficient number of men for Christian work. In these non-Christian lands many young men have a hold upon Christianity, but,

generally speaking, Christianity does not have a powerful hold upon them. Wherever in my visits to the colleges of Asia I found a student upon whom the Spirit
of God laid His mighty hand, I found a student who
was eager to enter upon the service of his fellow men,
and, therefore, willing to face the hardships, opposition, and sacrifice involved.

If I may mention another reason why we are not
raising up this army more rapidly and using it more ex-
tensively, I should say it is the lack of adequate efforts
and measures to secure and to use more workers. Those
churches and missions which have given most thought
to this problem are the churches and missions which
have raised up the largest number of effective workers.

What can be done to meet the difficulties to which
attention has been called, and to raise up this army?
In the first place, there should be a comprehensive and
thoroughgoing study of this question and a statesmanlike policy with reference to meeting the need. It should
be comprehensive, in the sense of taking into view, as
the Jesuits have done, the whole world. It should be
comprehensive, in a second sense, in that it embraces
the generation for the serving of which God holds us
responsible. Let the policy grapple with the whole generation, and not simply with emergencies. It should be
a statesmanlike policy, in the sense that it takes account
of all other forces in the Church of Christ at work on
the mission fields, thus avoiding duplicating or over-

lapping. So the Church should look down through the years, and so lay her plans as to bring up the forces to meet the needs of the world of our own day.

A second thing which is exceedingly important is that we greatly enlarge and strengthen the Christian educational work. I have had the privilege of visiting nearly all the hundreds of Christian colleges and high schools of the so-called non-Christian lands. I know of no colleges which have had a larger fruitage in respect to furnishing the right kind of Christian workers than some of these. There should be expended on them within the next ten years a large sum of money toward adding plants here and endowment there, strengthening the teaching force here, improving the equipment there. I believe that men of large financial ability and large outlook will respond far more generously to a plan which seems adequate to do the work which God has assigned to our generation, than to one which is obviously insufficient to meet the need and opportunity.

I am even more convinced that we should add to the force of workers in these colleges than that we should expand their material equipment. This is the last part of the world mission of Christianity that should be undermanned. It is poor economy to put up large institutional plants and underman them to the point that they fall short of productive investments. It has seemed to me that the staff of workers was often so overburdened with the technical work of teaching, which ought,

for the honor of Christ, to be kept up to scholarly standards, that they were not able to give the time that they
desired to give to the most vital part—touching the lives
of the students. We must add to the force of educational missionaries.

The staffs of such institutions should be increased to
such an extent that in every college and school the
teacher will have enough time to think, to grasp the
problems, to pray, to do much personal work, to impress the students deeply. I visited the college of Dr.
C. W. Mateer, in the Shantung Province, some years ago.
He and Mrs. Mateer had started that Christian college
about thirty years before the time of my visit. I learned
that every graduate of that institution had become a Christian before graduation, and that the large majority had
entered some form of Christian work as a life work.
Later, I found one or more of these graduates on the
teaching staff of nearly every important mission college
of China. When I asked Dr. Mateer the secret of the
wonderful influence of the college, he replied: "My wife
and I early came to the conclusion that we, together,
could not deeply impress more than sixty students. And
so we deliberately kept down the number of students."
The yield that followed would seem to have proved the
wisdom of their practice.

We should never cease to mention with gratitude the
name of Miss Eliza Agnew, who, within forty years,
sent out from her Christian girls' school in Ceylon 600

graduates as Christians, of whom over 200 entered what we should call distinctively Christian callings. She always gave personal attention to the individual student.

In India I met a man who made a profound impression upon me. Later, I learned that not infrequently he spent long hours—on one occasion, the whole night—in intercession for workers. A friend of mine went out from Oxford to India and became absorbed in executive work. He wrote me sometime ago: "I have decided to change my method; I am going to spend a large section of my time this year with a little group of men." The size of the group, I may say, was twelve. I heard from him, toward the close of the year, that the fires of God were burning in the lives of those men.

The greatest work of the missionary is the making of missionaries. In no other way can he so multiply himself. What a work was accomplished by the men who influenced for Christ such workers as Moses Kya, of the Sandwich Islands; Tiyo Soga and Bishop Crowther, of Africa; the great Sheshadri; the converted Brahman, Banurji, of Calcutta; Chatterjea, of the Punjab; and Pundita Ramabai, of Western India; the Brothers Meng, in North China, and Pastor Shen, the worker of the London Missionary Society; Miyagawa, of Osaka, and Honda and Uemura, of Tokyo. Lives like these are not the product of foreign money and intellectual culture alone— they are the gift of God through the example, the training, and the spiritual nurture of Christian missionaries and nationals.

Moreover, the student Christian movements in the non-Christian countries should be strongly supported. The Young Men's and Young Women's Christian Associations in the colleges of Asia and other non-Christian parts of the world are not engaged in a self-appointed task. These movements were planted by the missionaries and nationals in response to the initiative of the students or their teachers. The object of these Christian movements is to help evangelize the students, and lay upon them the burden for evangelizing their own people.

The methods employed by these movements are those which have been most fruitful in the colleges of the West. The devotional, thorough study of the Bible is much emphasized. Among other methods promoted are personal work, evangelistic campaigns in the neighborhood, and the development of missionary interest. Special stress is laid on influencing strong students to devote their lives to Christian work as a life work. Hundreds of students in China, Japan, India, Ceylon, the Levant, and throughout Africa have already become volunteers. The means employed by the national committees to develop these movements are: conferences for the deepening of the spiritual life and for training voluntary workers; the preparation and use of literature designed to help in the formation of right habits for the cultivation of the spiritual life, and to stimulate Christian effort; and the visits of expert secretaries, necessary even in Christian lands if the fires are to be kept burning and if the work is to be coördinated and brought into vital connection with similar movements of other countries. By means of the World's Student Christian Federation the student Christian movements of non-Christian lands are organically related to the Christian organizations of students all over the world.

Above all, there is need of far more prayer for the raising up and the thrusting forth of the army of native workers. This means is necessary to make all the other means effective. It is necessary to make them most largely productive. It is the means, and the only means, on which Christ has placed stress in connection with getting laborers. Any plan which neglects this factor is exceedingly superficial. Why leave unappropriated and unapplied the greatest force for the raising up and energizing of laborers and for calling into being and energizing spiritual movements?

VII. THE SUMMONS TO COÖPERATE

T HE WORLD MISSION OF CHRISTIAN-
ity has led the way in coöperation between Christian denominations, between nations, and between races.
The world context of this undertaking to make Jesus
Christ known and obeyed affords the necessary setting
in which to realize the true place and possibilities of
united fellowship, thinking, and action on the part of
His followers. Here we come to see that the dimensions
of the task are so vast, the issues at stake so great,
and the difficulties so baffling that nothing short of union
in plan, in organization, in intercession, and in sacrificial effort will avail.

The modern missionary age may be divided with respect to coöperation into three periods: first, the years
preceding the World Missionary Conference at Edinburgh in 1910; secondly, the years between that gathering and the Meeting of the International Missionary
Council held in Jerusalem in 1928; and thirdly, the new
epoch ushered in by this last momentous assembly. The

first period may be thought of as one in which experiments were initiated and ultimately multiplied into a large number of detached pieces of coöperative effort. These were scattered over the world. More were to be found in India than in any other field because of the better means of communication which even then obtained in that country. A wide range of programs and activities was represented—for example, evangelistic effort, educational work, medical work, producing and circulating literature, training workers, holding conferences, entering into agreements as to comity, and the launching of various auxiliary agencies in furtherance of common missionary objectives, especially at the home base. These many, varied, and more or less isolated coöperative projects were not in any way related to one another. Save in two or three home-base countries there was no effective organization or body responsible for bringing them into touch with one another.

The second period—that is, between Edinburgh and Jerusalem—had as its distinctive characteristic the creation and development in many parts of the world of agencies formed for the express purpose of inaugurating and fostering interdenominational, international, and interracial coöperation. At the beginning of the period there were but two Christian organizations for the purpose of uniting all the missionary forces in their respective countries—namely, those of Germany and North America. Eighteen years later, or at the time of the Jerusalem Meeting, there were twenty-six (now twenty-eight) Christian councils—fourteen in the countries or groups of countries which send missionaries, and twelve (now fourteen) in the countries or groups of countries to which missionaries are sent. As a rule each of these councils unites all the Protestant missionary agencies of the country. At the end of the Edinburgh Conference there was only the Continuation Committee appointed by that unofficial conference to carry forward some of the studies and other services initiated in connection with that gathering. The further that conference receded into the past, the further the committee it had created seemed to be from the sources of authority in all that pertains to missionary policy. The World War still further weakened its hold, notwithstanding the valuable services it was able to render. After the war it was succeeded by the International Missionary Council, which is the creation of and officially represents the twenty-eight national councils which in turn officially represent the church and missionary bodies of their respective fields. So now for the first time in the history of Christianity we have closely linked together both nationally and internationally the agents and agencies of the world mission of all Protestant Christendom. Moreover, during this second period coöperative or union projects, largely local or regional in scope, though at times also national, continued to multiply at an almost geometrical rate.

The third period upon which we entered at Jerusalem should prove to be much more significant in the realm of coöperative achievement than either of the preceding periods. It is the hope and belief of many responsible leaders that it may constitute a new epoch in which the implications of interdenominational and international coöperation may be taken much more seriously than ever before, and in which there may be realized the great results that ever attend genuine coöperation and unity. The periods which have gone before should be regarded as but preparatory to something which will far transcend anything hitherto achieved.

What is the design and significance of this extensive organization of the forces of the world-wide mission of the Christian faith? Why these nearly thirty national councils, and the International Missionary Council, the product of so much corporate thought, prayer, and sacrificial effort? Why the multiplication of union mission projects the world over? Why the various national federations of churches and recent movements toward the organic union of churches in different parts of Asia, Europe, Anglo-Saxon America, and Latin America? Were the striking developments in coöperation and unity designed to be simply ends in themselves? Or merely symbols of a wonderful and truly Christ-implanted idea? Rather have they not been called into being by the Ever-Living and Ever-Creative God Himself for great ends and great achievements?

It is highly significant that the growth in volume and momentum of this movement toward closer coöperation and unity synchronizes with the recent startling development of divisive movements and influences among men. It comes also at a time when the world mission is confronted with the greatest combination of difficulties which it has ever been called upon to meet. If ever Christian forces needed to present a united front to all that opposes, it is now. And yet the alarming fact is that it is entirely possible that the Christian forces may lose out through failure to combine, or through failure on the part of the Christians who have already united in various organizations to realize the implications of real coöperation and union and, therefore, to pay the sacrificial prices necessary. The most serious factor is not so much the divisive and other sinister forces which oppose the Christian Church but the divisions in the ranks of the Church itself and the apathy, indifference, and lack of heroic response with which Christians meet the summons to a far closer coöperation and unity. Without doubt our divisions are still our greatest handicap.

In many parts of the so-called non-Christian world our divisions are a serious stumblingblock in the way of the people of the country. The Christians in these lands find it impossible to reconcile the existence of so many denominations with the unity for which Christ prayed. Generally speaking, the churches in Asia, Africa, and Latin America, including both the nationals and the missionaries, are more ready for union and co-operation than those of the West. Let us look at the situation through the eyes of a few trusted nationals and missionaries.

The Right Reverend E. J. Palmer, formerly Bishop of Bombay, who has been one of the ablest advocates of Christian unity, thus expresses the view of many Indian Christians:

"Christian converts in a non-Christian land are bound to-gether by their sense of common separation from the great non-Christian system that they have left and their consequent overwhelming need of mutual support.

"The differences between the indigenous Christians seem as nothing when they think of their differences from the non-Christians around. Father Nehemiah Goreh, a Brahman con-vert who was a priest of my diocese, expressed it . . . years ago something like this: 'The difference between a Hindu who wor-ships a cow and an Indian Christian who has ceased to do so is so great that any theological differences there may be among Indian Christians make no impression on us.' " [1]

The Right Reverend V. S. Azariah, Bishop of Dorna-kal, who was the first Indian bishop, shows in the fol-lowing words how very necessary unity is as a witness before non-Christians in India:

"Thinking men ask why, while claiming loyalty to the One Christ we still worship separately, we still show exclusiveness in all the most sacred acts of our religion. The divisions confuse the thoughtful inquirer. 'Which church shall I join?' is often asked by such a convert. There have been many such 'little ones of Christ' who have been caused to stumble by our divisions. . . .

[1] Right Reverend E. J. Palmer, in *The International Review of Missions*, Vol. XVII, January, 1928, pp. 78 f.

"There is still another—even more serious—danger in India. Through our divisions, we unconsciously become parties to the creation of caste churches. Caste is the bulwark of Hinduism. This religion, as was told me by one of its great exponents, does not stand for doctrinal belief, it stands for a life. It is very accommodating in religious practices; it is relentless only in the demands of caste. By caste men are placed in water-tight compartments. Beyond the caste circle there is no real social life, no inter-dining, and certainly no intermarriage. There is no worse force in the whole world that operates for separating man from man, and creating jealousy, suspicion, and strife between communities, than this hydra-headed monster, caste. In such a land there is being planted, by the grace of God, a Divine Society, which is meant to be one, which was created by God to be one, and whose one characteristic worship is—by the ordinance of its Divine Master—participation in one common sacred Food. Division in this Society means exclusive communions and severed fellowship, and produces all the worst effects of the Hindu caste system." [2]

Bishop Azariah, in speaking at the Lausanne Conference on Faith and Order, also gave the following expression of his conviction:

"Unity may be theoretically a desirable ideal in Europe and America, but it is vital to the life of the Church in the mission field. The divisions of Christendom may be a source of weakness in Christian countries, but in non-Christian lands they are a sin and a scandal." [3]

One of the ablest Chinese theological professors, in commenting on the outstanding difficulties which Chris-

[2] Right Reverend V. S. Azariah, in *Faith and Order, Proceedings of the World Conference, Lausanne, August 3-21, 1927*, pp. 492, 494 (Garden City: Doubleday, Doran & Co., 1928).
[3] *Ibid.*, p. 495.

tians have placed in the way of non-Christians in China, says:

"Before we can win the peoples of the world by teaching them the love of Christ, we must set an example to them how we love one another within the Christian fold. To me the significance of the brief sojourn of the Master on this earth was to teach us, among many other things, the supreme value and necessity of fellowship.

"Christ's prayer for His disciples was not for their individual success or individual achievement, but for unity of and love of the group. Love and unity were indeed the two cornerstones of the Christian Church. The Church grew out of fellowship. It was carried on by love. . . .

"We who are in China look at the enormous divisions within the Christian Church with mingled emotions and different reactions. Some of us are dazed at the innumerable divisions into which the Christian Church has been officially broken and are astonished to see how intense is the unforgiving spirit and lack of Christian tolerance of Western civilization over certain religious issues.

"The non-Christian world to-day has an equal access to the facts of the history of the Christian Church, for the last 2,000 years, as we have ourselves. It sees for itself how we Christians have treated one another, and this is by far the strongest weapon it has by which to attack the very citadel of our endeavor.

"If all Western denominationalism is taken out of China, there may arise a Chinese denominationalism, no better and no worse than that which is now in the West.

"But for all that, those who have eyes to see the tremendous needs of Christ in China can never fail to realize what a united church, a truly church-centered fellowship, dominated by Christlike love, would mean to China. Theological differences, factional interests, and personal preferences—how big they loom before our eyes when we forget about Jesus and His teachings about God as the Father of all." [4]

[4] Timothy T. Lew, in *The Student World*, Vol. XX, pp. 105 f.

In the *Message of the Church*, prepared by the Commission presided over by Dr. C. Y. Cheng, the Moderator of the Church of Christ in China, also General Secretary of the National Christian Council, and presented at the last great National Christian Conference in Shanghai, is the following statement which voices the general feeling and belief of the Christian leaders throughout that field:

"We Chinese Christians who represent the various leading denominations express our regret that we are divided by the denominationalism which comes from the West. We are not unaware of the diverse gifts through the denominations that have been used by God for the enrichment of the Church. Yet we recognize fully that denominationalism is based upon differences, the historical significance of which, however real and vital to the missionaries from the West, is not shared by us Chinese. Therefore denominationalism, instead of being a source of inspiration, has been and is a source of confusion, bewilderment, and inefficiency. We recognize also most vividly the crying need of the Christian salvation of China to-day, and we firmly believe that it is only the united church that can save China, for our task is great and enough strength can only be attained through solid unity." [5]

Prof. D. D. T. Jabavu, a well-known leader among African Christians, who was prominent in the councils at Jerusalem, in the following words calls attention to what a stumblingblock the divisions among Christians are in South Africa:

"Another mistake concerns the perpetuation of denominationalism. It is regrettable that the old tribal divisions should

[5] C. Y. Cheng, in *The Message of the Church*, Report of Commission III, The National Christian Conference, Shanghai, May 2-11, 1922, p. 2 (Shanghai: Office of the Committee on Arrangements, n.d.).

be again cross-divided by an extraneous sectarianism with the genesis of which the Africans had nothing to do. One outcome of this religious separatism is that the indigenous races have taken these divisions more seriously than did their authors; and the unnecessary emphasis laid on them by some missionaries has produced lively antagonism among the newly-born Christians. This has made it harder to convert the heathen, because when these are visited by rival mission bands they inevitably ask: 'How many Gods are there? Which God are we asked to believe?'

"The overlapping of missionary work due to denominationalism produces some absurdities. For instance, in a village like Nancefield, near Johannesburg, containing only about five thousand natives, there are as many as thirty-four different Gospel bells or wagon-hoops ringing at eleven o'clock of a Sunday morning; and in the Pretoria Location there are sixty-five places of worship!" [6]

The Right Reverend James Henry Linton, Bishop in Persia, writes as follows:

"The strong desire for national unity has most naturally found its parallel in the active efforts towards unity in the Church. At the conference in Isfahan one Persian Christian said, 'You missionaries compose your differences, and we Persians will soon have a united church.' It is that sort of feeling among Persian Christians which makes missionaries feel keenly the sin of disunion. Unity is a vital matter affecting the very life of the Church, and is an immediate essential if the Church is to become an energising organism in the new Persia which is emerging from the chaos of ages." [7]

Dr. E. Stanley Jones, in the light of wide observation, thus expresses one of his deepest convictions:

[6] D. D. T. Jabavu, *The Segregation Fallacy and Other Papers* (*A Native View of Some African Inter-Racial Problems*), pp. 121 f. (Lovedale: Lovedale Institution Press, 1928).

[7] Right Reverend J. H. Linton, in *The Call for Christian Unity: The Challenge of a World Situation*, p. 161 (London: Hodder and Stoughton, 1930).

"The Gospel was intended to unite, to heal, to produce a brotherhood, to make the world one. That Gospel has often been so changed that, in fact, it has been used to divide, to wound, to produce innumerable sects, and to make the world more disrupted than ever. The curse of religion has been in its divisiveness. All the time there has been at the heart of our Gospel the fact that the Spirit founds life in love, therefore brings unity and produces brotherhood. . . .

"The churches that deliberately take the attitude of separation, or only grudgingly give way to the pressure for unity, forfeit their right to leadership in a world where to-day world tendencies are toward unity. In saving themselves they lose themselves." [8]

A failure to achieve closer coöperation and unity means the impoverishment of the leadership of this Christian enterprise. When the various Christian groups unite in an organization or program it makes the experience, knowledge, insight, statesmanship, creative personalities of all the groups more accessible and available for each. From the nature of the case, not to do so weakens each group. In one country in the Orient I found nineteen separate denominational theological seminaries with an aggregate of some 600 students. Two-thirds of these institutions were in or near one city, and most of the others were not very far distant. In answer to inquiries I was told that in only two or three of these seminaries was there in the chair of Church History a man who would be regarded as a front-line or highly competent authority on the subject. The situa-

[8] E. Stanley Jones, *The Christ of Every Road*, pp. 199, 205 (New York: The Abingdon Press, 1930). Copyright. Used by permission of the publishers.

tion with reference to the chair of Apologetics was not much more favorable. The result is that in each of these subjects, and doubtless it would be more or less true of certain others, the students of only a few denominations are having the benefit of the best instruction. This means that the future leadership of the churches in this field will in so far suffer. The same principle applies with reference to other kinds of institutions of learning and within other spheres of the Christian program and activity. Such situations are to be found in countries both in the Orient and in the Occident and must be met in some instances by several denominations' uniting in one institution, in others by uniting in a common system in which workers and facilities will be shared or interchanged. In any country there is only a limited number of really first-rate scholars or authorities. Why should their unique contribution and influence be confined to a small group of one communion when by well-wrought-out coöperative arrangements, if a plan involving organic unity is not practicable, these personalities can be made much more widely available? Such plans, affording as they do a more adequate outlet or opportunity for a man's powers, will secure more of the ablest and most highly equipped men for important positions in the work of the Church.

A practice which impoverishes the leadership of the Church also results in impoverishing the membership.

If the preachers, the teachers, the editors are weak or inadequately furnished, surely the rank and file of the Christians who look to them for guidance, upbuilding, and inspiration must suffer. Professor Moffatt, in writing about his contacts with not a few ministers in the Middle Western States of America, commented on their "thin libraries." I have had similar experiences in connection with inquiries as to the mental equipment and resources of the Christian leaders in many countries. It is pathetic to think what so many of the Christians of the younger churches, as well as of the older churches, are losing in enrichment of life, enlargement of view, and sense of belonging to a great fellowship, as a result of a system which so contracts the Christian leadership to which these Christians are exposed.

In some countries there is grave danger that the failure to pool or unite the spiritual penetration, the thought power, and the gifts of strategy and statecraft of the various churches may result in letting the initiative pass out of the hands of the Christians into the hands of the antireligious and other inimical forces. In Japan, and in other parts of the Far East, the inflow of the works of the materialistic school of communism caught the Christian leaders off their guard. The same has been all too true among leaders in the United States in face of the teachers and writers representing the behaviorist psychology and the exponents of the humanism which denies the superhuman. At a time of so much confusion of thought, when there has been and still is need of affording a clear authentic lead, it is an unfortunate fact that the Christians, as a result of lack of a wider fellowship in thought, have at times been thrown on the defensive.

Evidence is not wanting in any field that many lose confidence in Christian missions because of our all-too-many divisions. Whether rightly or wrongly, they believe that there is still unnecessary duplication of effort and failure to concentrate forces to best advantage as a result of too extreme denominational and national emphasis and practice. Some who hold this view are to be found among present donors; many more, among possible large donors. Apart from men and women of means, this also represents the attitude of a large number of thoughtful people. On the other hand, wherever the world mission gives the impression of a united, aggressive movement, based on a clearly defined, concrete, coöperative program, confidence is restored and maintained.

In the fields where there is wanting a genuinely inter-denominational and international program of coöperation and union, the Christian cause fails to receive the contribution of smaller countries and communions. On the other hand, where there is such a comprehensive program and organization or fellowship, the representatives of these smaller units often become principal formative factors in shaping policies and moving spirits in putting such policies into effect. This is well illustrated in the League of Nations and in the International Labor Office, where expert knowledge and experience and sheer merit often put men from little countries into positions of major responsibility and influence. Again, this is seen in the entire history of the World's Student Christian Federation, which from its foundation placed the various national student Christian movements on an equality— whether they were in large countries or small, whether these movements were old or young, whether they represented so-called backward races or advanced, whether their membership was made up largely of members of the larger Christian communions or of smaller or more obscure bodies. The result has been that at times the most prophetic leadership has come from most unexpected quarters of the world. The experience of the International Missionary Council confirms the same point. At its Jerusalem Meeting no man made a more valuable contribution than the young missionary, Dr. Kraemer, from the out-of-the-way field of Java, formerly of Holland. The Society of Friends, although one of the smallest of all Christian bodies, furnishes some of the most creative and dynamic spiritual personalities, the outreach of whose ministry might be greatly circumscribed were it not for coöperative arrangements which integrate them with the Christians of other names.

Unless much more effective coöperation and unity be brought about in the period right before us, the Christian forces will find it impossible to meet great opportunities and great dangers. Certain opportunities and demands are so vast and baffling that it is impossible for denominations and nationalities working singly and separately to meet them. What is everybody's business turns out to be nobody's business; or at the best, earnest fractional and detached efforts are put forth with relatively small effect.

The need of a more adequate Christian literature program for China may serve as an apt illustration. Notwithstanding the good work accomplished in this field in spots, as it were, by some of the most eminent missionaries and Chinese scholars who have ever lived, and despite the helpful activities of various denominational and interdenominational societies within the scope of the material and human forces at their disposal, there is general agreement among observers, both within China and outside, including Chinese leaders, missionaries, and mission board officers and members as well as special students of mission problems, that we are falling far short of meeting the tremendous situation. The Christian agencies are teaching vast numbers to read but are leaving it all too much to the non-Christian and even antireligious elements to supply the reading matter. Moreover, it is not alone the numerical aspect of the subject which causes concern. Here is the spectacle of a fourth of the human race being rapidly exposed to all the currents of the modern world. Their coming leaders by the hundreds of thousands have largely cast off the sanctions, standards, and principles which have guided or controlled their ancestors and are without adequate guidance and vital energies to shape character and afford the life abundant.

What hope is there of meeting the insatiable demand for mental food and the need for spiritual light unless the all-too-divided Christian forces have a masterly, united plan to which they will lend adequate support in money and some of their ablest personalities? There should be a thoroughly representative and otherwise fully qualified body which would have power to do five things: (1) survey and evaluate with courage and candor the existing Christian literature available in various dialects and for various groups; (2) discover the unfilled gaps or needs and determine the order in which these needs should be met; (3) search out the persons best qualified by experience and by literary ability to supply particular needs; (4) take initiative in the negotiations to have such persons lent or allocated for the work desired, including arrangements, financial and otherwise, to make conditions favorable for the best literary work; (5) draw on the experience of other lands, East and West, regarding the largest and most satisfactory introduction and use of the literature. Parts of such a program are now in use in certain fields. Considering limitation of resources, one of the best illustrations of what can be done by such comprehensive co-operative measures is that of the Committee on Christian Literature for Moslems (of all lands) having its headquarters in Cairo. Another illustration is that of the India Literature Fund of the National Christian Council of India, Burma, and Ceylon. There with very meager financial backing but with pooling of experience, insight, and influence, results of such character have been secured as to make absolutely convincing the wisdom of a policy which would increase on a large scale the resources placed at the disposal of the committee.

Another situation which demands practical unity and coöperation in program and execution of program unless the Christian cause is to lose out—at least in the sense of falling far short of realizing its possibilities—is in the realm of Christian higher and secondary school education in fields such as China, India, and Japan, and in not a few smaller countries. In each of these fields, as well as elsewhere, there are individual institutions, colleges, so-called universities, and secondary schools in the maintenance of which two or more denominations have united and which demonstrate advantages of such coöperative effort, but taking the Christian educational work in a given country as a whole conditions are far from satisfactory. There is needed a united program and policy which will be accepted by all the Christian bodies concerned and in connection with which the financial and other implications are recognized and accepted with seriousness and determination. Failing this, not only will the Christian educational work lose its supreme opportunity, but the entire Christian movement thereby will also suffer irreparable loss. In none of these lands can the Christian churches begin to keep pace quantitatively with the vast and ever-expanding government and secular systems of education. They can, however, excel qualitatively, provided the Christian bodies unite with full heart, conviction, and sacrificial devotion. It will probably mean concentrating in the years immediately before us on fewer colleges than now exist; also on developing to a high degree of intellectual and spiritual efficiency and fruitage a system of union secondary schools. It will call for a unifying and supervising board, and in certain countries which are helping to support the system there will be coöperating groups. Giving largest effect to such a plan will involve, it may be, some difficult adjustments, personal, denominational, sectional, or national, but without such sacrificial and truly united action the cause of Christ will miss the day of its visitation. It is hoped that the report of the Higher Educational Commission which has recently visited India, and of the one so soon to visit Japan, will point the way to meeting these great situations; also that in China, before it is too late, there may be evolved a plan, conserving and supplementing all that is best in the report of the Burton Commission, which will afford a unity transcending present differences.

The question of religious liberty has in recent years been thrust into prominence in the Far East, the Near East, Eastern Asia, and different parts of Africa, not to mention other areas. This state of things is due not only to the attitude of certain governments but also to the activities of antireligious movements, and it imperatively demands united consideration on the part of the Christian and, it may be, other religious bodies.

The reason certain great evils are not being grappled with successfully is lack of united, wise, and heroic action on the part of the various churches. Typical of such evils are, for example, the corrupting movies of America and Europe now so widely exhibited in Asia, Africa, Latin America, and the island world. Others, such as the opium curse and the drink evil, are world problems and call for world-wide collaboration on the part of the Christian and other constructive forces.

The greatest common enemy of all religions is the prevailing and spreading secular civilization. This secular world is a unified world. Our best Christian thinkers among theologians, philosophers, psychologists, and educationalists are coming more and more to see the need of joining forces and working much more in concert to meet the secularist position.

Incomparably the most serious aspect of continued divisions and aloofness among Christians, and of failure to give unmistakable impression of unity not only in name and spirit but also in Christlike attitude and service, is that we rob the Christian religion of its mightiest apologetic. On the authority of Christ this triumphant apologetic is the one He had in mind when He prayed, "that they all may be one . . . that the world may believe." In this prayer He revealed that such unity or oneness is possible and obligatory. "Christ," as Bishop Brent said, voicing his dominant life conviction, "wills unity." Every extension of the visible fellowship of Christians will increase the power of the Church to witness to its Lord. If an unbelieving world in these days sees a growing unity in the international field and in other relations, and at the same time observes Christians of different communions, nationalities, and races unable to demonstrate that they love and trust one another enough to unite, what other conclusion can it form than that the Church has lost her way and vacated her spiritual leadership?

What is the secret of the most fruitful coöperation and of triumphant unity? To begin with, there must be apostles of reconciliation. They must be men with the contagious power and the staying power which comes to a man who has a sense of divine mission. At the back of every great advance in the drawing together of Christians in deeper understanding, mutual sacrifice, and constructive achievement has been a group. By advocacy, by example, and by all other efforts its members have built bridges of communication and mutual helpfulness between groups which had been formerly isolated from

each other, or perhaps had misunderstood and opposed
each other.   Although ably supported by Christians of
every name and clime, Bishop Brent and Robert H.
Gardiner worked in a class by themselves in the extensive and intensive activities which culminated in the
Lausanne Conference on Faith and Order.   What does
not the recent union of the two largest churches in Scotland owe to well-nigh forty years of patient, far-sighted,
wise work of Principal Rainy and his colleagues.   The
splendid result achieved in bringing together the three
bodies that constituted the United Church of Canada
would never have been secured had it not been for the
labors of men like Dr. S. D. Chown, Dr. G. C. Pidgeon,
Dr. James Endicott, Principal Gandier, and Dr. W. T.
Gunn.   What an example in thoroughness, comprehension, toleration, and undiscourageable enthusiasm for a
cause has been set by Bishop Azariah, K. T. Paul, J. H.
Maclean, Bishop Palmer, Dr. J. J. Banninga, and not a
few others in the evolution of the church union movement
of South India.   The Church of Christ in China, which
binds together some fourteen or more bodies of Christians, likewise owes its existence to a little band, including such men as Dr. C. Y. Cheng, Dr. G. H. McNeur, Dr.
P. F. Price, and Dr. C. G. Sparham.   There must be multiplication of examples like these of men of catholic
mind, vision, constructive ability, tireless perseverance,
reverential regard for all that is good and true in the
past, and, above all, passionate desire to fulfill the

prayer of Christ. Their number need not be large at the beginning. Even one such apostle at the back of any sound, well-conceived, unselfish piece of coöperative work will find that his spirit becomes contagious.

Undergirding every project of unity and coöperation that will stand the strain and by its results demonstrate its beneficence, there must be thorough, broad-minded, courageous, conclusive thinking, especially shown in honest diagnosis of conditions, in counting the cost, and in grasping and applying guiding principles. From the nature of the case there must be not only independent thinking by individuals in solitude but also what is equally important, group or corporate thinking. In this connection I wish to recommend the attentive reading of the latest edition of the book by Mr. Basil Mathews and Mr. Harry Bisseker, *Fellowship in Thought and Prayer*.

It may be suggestive and helpful to state quite simply and concisely a few principles and also attitudes which, in many years devoted to helping unite Christians of all communions, nations, and races, in various international and world-wide organizations, one has found may be relied upon:

Interdenominationalism as contrasted with undenominationalism. It need not be pointed out that there is all the difference in the world between the two. What is needed is something with more vitality, power, and

richness than is possessed by vague, colorless, weak undenominationalism.

Maximums, not minimums. This does not involve
minimizing, evading, or obscuring differences but
transcending them.

Unselfishness. Not what each can get, but what
each can give—that is, how render the maximum of
service?

Humility. This is the secret of slaying pride, the
great enemy of triumphant unity—whether the pride be
personal, or of denomination, nationality, or race.
Christ emptied Himself.

Living in large dimensions—dominated by wide visions, exhibiting large-mindedness and large-hearted-
ness. This is the only hope of being saved from petti-
ness, narrowness, and unworthy motives.

Regarding difficulties as not to be yielded to, but
to be overcome. If Christ willed unity (and what
else, let it be reiterated, did His prayer for unity imply?), then difficulties are designed to facilitate and not
to hinder the secret of triumphant unity.

A constant study of priorities. Fruitful coöperation
and arrival at triumphant unity involves time and employment of certain processes. It is necessary all the
way, therefore, to be resolutely discovering first things
and placing them first—distinguishing also between es-
sentials and nonessentials.

Recognition of the Lordship of Christ. In all cases

of doubt or hesitation, the governing consideration must be the mind of Christ.

Another secret of achieving increasingly fruitful coöperation and enduring unity is that of honest, fearless, impartial evaluation of experiences. Some of the undertakings most needed in the direction of uniting Christian forces, undertakings inaugurated with a most promising outlook, have fallen short of expectations and been abandoned without any study of the causes of disappointing results for the purpose of overcoming them or profiting by them. Again, many union projects have become formal and lifeless, and are not justifying their existence. They are being allowed to drift along and become a stumblingblock in the way of the cause of Christian unity and coöperation; whereas if they were subjected to a thorough examination, the cause of the failure might be easily discovered and a period of successful experience be ushered in. At times, in the light of such investigation, the comparative failure of coöperative projects could be traced to a totally inadequate financial support. When this needed factor was supplied by the proper constituency, the enterprise developed into a marked success. Unsatisfactory experience in coöperative effort is often due to inadequate leadership. At times there has been a failure by one or more parties to the undertaking to play the game and do their proper part.

The leaders of union institutions and movements of

any kind must learn to pay what it costs to insure a really strong and helpful organization. A study of the national Christian councils and many educational, medical, and other kinds of union institutions which have been most successful, and the great value of which no one questions, reveals that in most cases the following factors afford a satisfactory explanation: (1) a strong, representative administrative committee with stated, unhurried meetings, at not too long intervals, with nearly all members attending, even if this involves the paying of expenses; (2) an able secretariat with an up-to-date headquarters office, but, as a rule, the staff spending most of their time in the field; (3) a well-thought-out financial policy accepted and supported by the constituency; (4) a forward-looking program; (5) projects which are regarded by the constituency as needed and important, and the work on them in each case strictly first class; (6) contact maintained with similar bodies elsewhere for the sake of receiving and imparting help; (7) the administrative committee regarding its powers as consultative and advisory, not legislative or mandatory—and in no sense considering itself a superboard; (8) a vivid sense of dependence on God. To reiterate one of these points, it should be stated that in the age-long history of the most successful Christian movements and institutions there has been discovered no substitute for bringing together for intimate fellowship, corporate thought, and united intercession the groups of men and women providentially set apart to administer great trusts. Those who do not after unselfish thought and prayer have a sense of being charged by God Himself with such responsibility had better yield their places to others; for it is my belief that it is just at this point that we find the cause of the comparative weakness, mediocrity, and unproductivity of many an organization that bears the Christian name. In the present overorganized state of Christianity few things would be more wholesome than to scrap not a little of the existing machinery, and reconstitute it so that it will indeed be a living organism.

Major emphasis must be placed upon the absolute necessity of mutual sacrifice as a vital part of the secret of Christ-appointed union and coöperation. If its achievement has not necessitated genuine sacrifice on the part of the various groups concerned, we may doubt whether it has been initiated by God. This principle inheres in the very genius of Christian union. Christ taught His followers that, in setting out to build a new structure, they should count the cost. He knew that it would be costly. To judge from the context of His teaching and of His own life, He wanted them to count the cost with reference to paying. He "for the joy that was set before Him endured the Cross, despising shame, and hath sat down at the right hand of the throne of God."

To bring together into a vital spiritual solidarity the Christians of various ecclesiastical backgrounds and of many lands and races in the world mission of Christianity is preëminently a superhuman undertaking. Christ was familiar with all the difficulties involved. He pierced to the heart of the solution of the problem when He set the example to His followers for all time by giving Himself to prayer for this sublime object. He left no ground for doubt as to just where the secret lies.

VIII. THE SUMMONS OF THE LIVING MESSAGE

Prior TO THE EARLY YEARS OF this century the attitude of Christian workers toward the non-Christian religions was largely negative and unappreciative, at times militant and destructive. During the past two or three decades the attitude has become increasingly positive, constructive, sympathetic, and irenic but without compromise. Missionaries and other Christian scholars—for example, Dr. Farquhar in his *Heritage of India* series—have had a major part in bringing about the change. The Jerusalem Meeting of the International Missionary Council also made a great contribution, dealing as it did on a world-wide scale, as well as intensively, with the Christian life and message in relation to non-Christian systems of thought and life.

The Committee and officers of the Council, in planning for the meeting, arranged to have papers prepared by eminent authorities on the various non-Christian re-

ligions or systems—Hinduism, Buddhism (both Northern and Southern), Confucianism, Mohammedanism,
and secular civilization. These were carefully studied
by the delegates, and were also circulated in advance
throughout the world and made the basis of study and
discussion circles and open forums. The distinguishing
characteristic of these papers and of their world-wide
consideration was the new approach to the subject. The
writers of the papers and the leaders of the study and
discussion groups were asked to deal especially with
the values of the various non-Christian systems. This
did not mean that other aspects of the inquiry were
overlooked, but that, inasmuch as heretofore emphasis
had been placed on unfavorable features, it would
be well on this occasion to approach these faiths in a
more appreciative and constructive manner. It was
thought that this approach and temper were abundantly
justified by such words of Christ as

"I am come not to destroy but to fulfill."
"My Father worketh hitherto and I work."
"He that is not against us is for us."

Just as the word "sharing" and the process it connotes came to be one of the two or three great conceptions which will ever be associated with the Jerusalem
Meeting, so this word "values" and the point of view,
attitude, and spirit which it signifies will in years to
come be thought of in connection with that creative
gathering.

Shortly before the Jerusalem conference delegates of some of the countries on the continent of Europe became solicitous lest this centering of attention on the consideration of the values of non-Christian faiths, and a possible neglect to give sufficient thought to the absolute uniqueness of Christianity, might result in a dangerous syncretism. They accordingly requested an opportunity to meet with the officers of the International Missionary Council to consider the matter. The request was gladly granted and a meeting of nearly all the Continental delegates with the officers was held in Cairo preceding the Jerusalem gathering. The result was reassuring, and it was agreed that the grounds of concern on the part of the group should be presented at the Jerusalem Meeting.

The subject of the message was given the first place in the program at Jerusalem. The entire conference at the outset devoted two extended open-forum sessions to its consideration. The conference also broke into sectional meetings in order that separate groups might deal more intensively with the Christian message in relation to the different non-Christian systems. Then a Findings Committee, with the Archbishop of York and Dr. Robert E. Speer as co-chairmen, devoted much time to formulating the report which near the close of the conference received the careful attention of all the delegates. Because of the primary importance of the subject the chairman suggested that the vote be deferred

until the following day that there might be ample time
for each delegate to devote further prayerful study to
the report.

As the Archbishop of York read the Message aloud to
the whole Council a sense of wonder and of solemn joy
pervaded the gathering. The delegates saw that here was
a great word for the present age. While it bore the
limitations inevitable to every human attempt to express the divine, the Message was so real in its Christian experience, so rich and so daring in its content, so
deeply rooted in the heritage of the past, and so fully
alive to the summons of the present, that it came as a
God-given lead to the Christian forces in this new day.

When the vote was taken it was unanimous. It is
highly significant that this body of men and women of
fifty-one nations, representing so many races, ecclesiastical backgrounds, and schools of thought, found it possible to unite on the statement of the Christian message
in relation to the non-Christian systems of thought and
life. Not by evading, or by compromising, or by ignor-
ing difficulties, but by transcending them this company
of leaders of the world mission reached a unity not tenta-
tive, or hesitant, but whole-hearted, living, and confi-
dent. They arrived at this oneness not by losing touch
with reality but by finding a higher and more inclusive
reality.

What is the significance of this great result? It lies
in the affording of a message which is a timely and sat-

isfying apologetic for this day. In our past attitude toward the non-Christian systems of faith and life, we have doubtless been prone to fix attention on their weaknesses, shortcomings, even errors and stains. Consequently there has been, to a greater extent than many have realized, a widespread skepticism and dissatisfaction which might be expressed thus: "We quite understand that when Christ is set in contrast over against the failures and sins of other faiths, they suffer by comparison; but, if we only knew all that is noble, true, beautiful, and helpful in them, it might be shown that, while Christ would still be seen to be desirable, He would not appear absolutely essential." It was to meet this very questioning that the plan used in the preparation of the papers, as well as in their consideration before Jerusalem and in the discussions at Jerusalem, was adopted and carried out. What was the result? It was overwhelmingly proved that the more open-minded, honest, just, and generous we were in dealing with the non-Christian faiths, the higher Christ loomed in His absolute uniqueness, sufficiency, supremacy, and universality. More than ever before, we saw Him as One other than all the rest—other than the saints and sages of ancient Hinduism, other than Buddha, Confucius, and Mohammed, other than Moses and St. Paul—"strong among the weak, erect among the fallen, believing among the faithless, clean among the defiled, living among the dead." In all the many months of fresh study of the values of non-Christian systems across the world, or the comprehensive and luminous sharing of knowledge, spiritual insight, and personal experience at Jerusalem, nothing was discovered or took place which would tend in the least to invalidate the claim and belief that in Christ we have the Central Figure of the Ages and the Eternities, the Fountain Head of Spiritual Life, the unfailing Source of Creative Energy, the World's Redeemer, the Desire of All Nations.

It is here that the Message of the Jerusalem Council finds its source. After outlining the broad background of the trends of life to-day the Message goes on:

"Our message is Jesus Christ. He is the revelation of what God is and of what man through Him may become. In Him we come face to face with the Ultimate Reality of the universe; He makes known to us God as our Father, perfect and infinite in love and in righteousness; for in Him we find God incarnate, the final, yet ever-unfolding, revelation of the God in whom we live and move and have our being.

"We hold that through all that happens, in light and in darkness, God is working, ruling and overruling. Jesus Christ, in His life and through His death and resurrection, has disclosed to us the Father, the Supreme Reality, as almighty Love, reconciling the world to Himself by the Cross, suffering with men in their struggle against sin and evil, bearing with them and for them the burden of sin, forgiving them as they, with forgiveness in their own hearts, turn to Him in repentance and faith, and creating humanity anew for an ever-growing, ever-enlarging, everlasting life.

"The vision of God in Christ brings and deepens the sense of sin and guilt. We are not worthy of His love; we have by our own fault opposed His holy will. Yet that same vision which brings the sense of guilt brings also the assurance of

pardon, if only we yield ourselves in faith to the spirit of
Christ so that His redeeming love may avail to reconcile us to
God.

"We reaffirm that God, as Jesus Christ has revealed Him,
requires all His children, in all circumstances, at all times,
and in all human relationships, to live in love and righteousness for His glory. By the resurrection of Christ and the
gift of the Holy Spirit God offers His own power to men that
they may be fellow workers with Him, and urges them on to
a life of adventure and self-sacrifice in preparation for the
coming of His Kingdom in its fullness." [1]

The Jerusalem Message, as it is known, has come with
power to all parts of the world. In university centers,
in companies of thoughtful laymen, and among the more
alert and profound of the clergy and of the editors of
the religious press, it is regarded as affording a much-
needed and convincing apologetic. Discerning leaders among the missionary forces of the churches are
seeking to secure for the Message earnest attention. It
has found its way into many languages, and literally
millions of copies have been circulated. Discussion
groups and open forums, using it as the subject for
special study, have been organized in all parts of the
world. Conferences and retreats are being held with
the Jerusalem Message as the central theme. Hundreds
of ministers in different denominations are making it
the basis for a series of sermons.[2]

[1] *The Christian Life and Message in Relation to Non-Christian Systems of Thought and Life.* The Jerusalem Meeting of the International
Missionary Council, March 24–April 8, 1928, Vol. I, p. 402 (New York:
The International Missionary Council, 1928). Copyright. Used by permission.
[2] The Message is reproduced in full as an appendix to this volume.

The officers of the International Missionary Council are making the further consideration of the Message a subject of major emphasis. They have felt the need of exploring still more deeply the relation of the profoundest and freshest modern thought in theology, philosophy, psychology, and science to the truth that is in Christ. On their initiative, therefore, conferences of younger as well as older professors and other Christian scholars have been held in North America, in Great Britain, and on the Continent with this as the central theme. A similar meeting with a limited group representing both Oriental and Occidental countries is now being projected. The special aim is to arrive at general agreement as to the real issues which concern the Christian faith as it confronts the modern world, in order that thought, prayer, and effort may be more effectively brought to bear upon them.

The governing and all-pervading purpose of the world mission is the release of its vital message. Expressed quite simply, this governing objective is to make Jesus Christ heard, known, trusted, loved, and obeyed in the whole range of individual life and in all human relationships. This is the work most needed, relatively most neglected, incomparably most important, most highly multiplying, and most enduring. As the Jerusalem Message says:

"Herein lies the Christian motive; it is simple. We cannot live without Christ and we cannot bear to think of men living without Him. We cannot be content to live in a world that is un-Christlike. We cannot be idle while the yearning of His heart for His brethren is unsatisfied.

"Since Christ is the motive, the end of Christian missions fits in with that motive. Its end is nothing less than the production of Christlike character in individuals and societies and nations through faith in and fellowship with Christ the living Saviour, and through corporate sharing of life in a divine society.

"Christ is our motive and Christ is our end. We must give nothing less, and we can give nothing more." [3]

While the methods employed may vary in different countries, in different kinds of communities, and in dealing with different groups, there are certain guiding principles, personal attitudes, vital processes, and dynamic factors which are universal in their significance and application. Bearing all this in mind, what in these days throughout the world field should characterize the larger release of the vital message?

The larger release of the living message has as its precursor and accompaniment larger desire—larger desire to share the inestimable blessings which we through Christ have received. Therefore, it is a longing to share Christ Himself. We have nothing so satisfying, precious, and enduring—nothing which will compare with Him. It is a governing passion to see Christ manifested and His reign extended. When this burning desire does not exist, it can be generated; where it has become weak, it can be intensified. The secret is two-

[3] *Ibid.*, pp. 406 f.

fold: meditation on human need and meditation on God. Let any one dwell in thought on the poverty, weakness, loneliness, sense of burden, and atrophy of lives without Christ, and he is strangely constituted if it does not awaken within him strong and unselfish desire, outbreaking into prayer and effort, that the living message may be brought to them. And let one think earnestly and reverently on God—who He is, what His character is, as shown in Christ, what His disposition is, what His ways have been, what His resources are; must he not be abnormal if he does not with pure and holy passion lend himself to the central governing purpose of the world mission—that of extending Christ's rule over all life and all life's relationships? Not until more Christians come to know in personal experience what enabled the great missionary to the Moslems, Raymond Lull, to say, "I have one passion: it is He, it is He," will there be generated the spiritual energies necessary to insure the world-wide release of the Christian message.

The adequate liberation of the living message necessitates far larger plans on the part of all the churches and mission agencies. As we think not only of geographical fields and the numerical aspects of world evangelization, but also and even more of the areas of life and human relations to be brought under the sway of Christ, how pitiably inadequate our plans are! How unworthy of the announced designs, the all-inclusive program, and the wondrous redemptive and life-abounding provision of our divine Lord! Christian leaders to-day should seek in their planning and sacrificial effort to emulate the great missionary apostle. He announced as his purpose to "present every man perfect in Christ." Notice the extensive aspect of his unselfish ambition— "present every man"; likewise note its intensive emphasis —"perfect in Christ." A splendid illustration of Christlike vision and sweep in planning is that of the Kingdom of God Movement now in progress in Japan. In their effort to quadruple the number of Christians in that country during three years the National Christian Council, with the prophetic leadership of Dr. Kagawa, have mapped out the whole country; set up coöperating committees in each prefecture; perfected special arrangements to reach certain groups, such as the peasants, factory working men and women, the miners, the fishing folk; instituted measures for training thousands of voluntary lay workers; launched a large publication program; and laid a mine of prayer. They have already demonstrated that it is easier to rally the forces to an impossible undertaking than to one that is easy and involves walking by sight only. The plan announced by the China Inland Mission not long ago to secure and send into the interior provinces 200 new missionaries and to obtain their necessary support, and this in the face of overwhelming difficulties and grave perils, and when most mission boards have been reducing staff or trying simply to hold their own, is another example of spacious planning for the larger release of the absolutely essential, life-giving message. It should be added that the plan was wrought out after prolonged and most searching study and consultation and much corporate intercession. Some boards and churches which have been so much occupied with effecting agonizing cuts and with exhausting efforts to avert deficits may well consider whether it may not be necessary to have more expansive plans if they are to call forth any heroism or sacrifice.

If the message is to come to men with most effect, there is need for larger comprehension on the part of those who proclaim it, as well as of those who lay plans for its release. This involves a better understanding of the field—that is, of the people to be reached—their antecedents, background, environment, and social and economic condition; a greater awareness of the changed psychology almost everywhere; an acquaintance with men's battleground of temptation; a knowledge of their unanswered questions about life, morals, and religion; and a recognition of the forces that are arrayed against Christ. Very special study should be made of favoring conditions and factors. Those that are not against Christ should be claimed for Him. "All are yours; and ye are Christ's; and Christ is God's." Chiefly and supremely, all those who would see the living message released should ever bear in mind that Christ is the message and that He must speak the word that causes conscience to be afraid and that energizes the will to take the step between knowing and doing.

There must be the larger message. Let it be re-iterated, our message, as Jerusalem said, is Christ. It is something objective—an Ever-Living Personality. Not a new Christ, for "He is the same yesterday, to-day, yea and forever," but a larger Christ, larger in the sense that there are so many more living now than ever before who have had experience of Him, and so many more communities now than ever before, the world over, which have furnished demonstrations of His trans-forming power in human relations. We go forth to pro-claim a Gospel which offers abundant life, even to those in the gloomiest slums of Western cities, among the untouchables and unapproachables of India, and in the abodes of cruelty and shame in darkest Africa. It is a Gospel which summons to a life more adventurous and more demanding than any other known to mankind. In making His Gospel difficult, Christ has made it tri-umphant.

The releasing of a living message—one which will lay hold of the people of to-day—calls for larger adapta-tions of means and methods. Christian workers every-where will profit greatly from a study of the spiritual awakenings and campaigns of evangelism of other gen-erations—for example, the Wesleyan revival of the eighteenth century, the mighty evangelistic activities of Finney in the early part of the nineteenth century, and

the wonderful experiences of Moody on both sides of
the Atlantic in the latter part of that century.   Possibly
quite as rewarding will be conversing with living witnesses of the meetings of Henry Drummond in the British Isles, America, and Australia, the nation-wide student
evangelistic campaigns conducted by representatives of
the World's Student Christian Federation in different
countries of Asia, North Africa, Europe, and North
America during the first decade and a half of this century, the Taiko Dendo or memorable evangelistic campaign in Japan several years ago, the remarkable revival which broke out on the Island of Nias in the Netherlands Indies, and the Men and Religion Campaign in
North American cities twenty years ago.   Most instructive and stimulating would it be to learn of such present-
day experiences in evangelistic and apologetic work as
that of Stanley Jones in India and South America, John
Mackay in all parts of Latin America, the Archbishop
of York at Oxford University, and, above all, the Kingdom of God Movement in Japan.   These and other similar
experiences in confronting men of different nations and
social groups with Christ and the implications of His
Gospel will abound in suggestions and mightily stimulate faith.   But to insure the most fruitful results workers in each country, in laying their plans for the presenta-
tion of the Christian message, must seek to adapt means
and methods to the particular field and group concerned.   In the light of study of various efforts, includ-

ing those mentioned above, and of careful consideration of changed conditions and of present-day requirements, I venture to emphasize certain points as applicable to-day in nearly all parts of the world.

It is desirable to take advantage of certain times and seasons—for example, the period culminating with Holy Week and the closing of the old and the opening of the new year. It is well to have the laws of association working for us as we seek to realize our high objective.

Concentrate all the forces on a given community, such as a university or a city. The campaigns of social evangelism waged in the capital city of Des Moines, Iowa, two successive years are a good illustration of what such concentrated effort makes possible.

Make much of retreats. The going apart of workers with the specific design to place themselves before God and to hear and heed His voice has never failed to yield great spiritual results as a preparatory process for fruitful evangelism.

Lay emphasis on religious education. This is of basic importance the world over, especially in any effort to achieve the largest and most enduring results among youth.

The whole Gospel should be preached. This includes not only the individual emphasis but also the social. They are integral parts of one Gospel. The practice of Kagawa, and the experience of some of the Old Testament prophets and of John the Baptist enforce the timeliness as well as the timelessness of this emphasis.

The group method so much used by Christ and by religious leaders across the centuries, down to the present day, has demonstrated its unique value in achieving the largest intensive and creative results. Dr. E. Stanley Jones with his Round Table has done much to commend this method in our time.

Great is the need of multiplying the number of apologetic voices and pens. Never were they more needed and so much in demand. It is alarming to see how few apologetic speakers and writers there are of such richness of intellectual background, insight, authentic experience of Christ, and power of interpretation as to command the intellectual and spiritual confidence of thoughtful and inquiring men of to-day. Whenever they are discovered means must be provided to make their gifts and powers widely available.

Much greater use may well be made of the printed page. The success of newspaper evangelism, first employed in Japan, has abundantly justified the use of it in other parts of the world. The leadership and material resources of Christian literature societies must be augmented that both in quality and in volume their productions may better serve the great evangelistic objective. The society of younger Japanese Christian scholars, recently formed for the purpose of better meeting the need in that country for apologetic and other Christian works of the highest order, has afforded a lead which might well be followed in other countries.

The deeper one penetrates into the secret of the most creative and aboundingly fruitful spiritual awakenings and movements to which we trace the marked expansion of vital Christianity, the more profound is the conviction that the releasing of such superhuman energies is the result of the intercession of men and women of prayer. One has been unable to discover an exception to this rule. So with unshakable conviction the chief emphasis, in the entire realm of ways and means, must be placed on this practice which was so central in the life and teachings of Christ Himself. In proportion to the reality and constancy of the prayer life of the Christians before, during, and following employment of all other means will be the extent and the transforming and enduring character of the results.

For the larger release of the living message the supreme need is that of infinitely greater resources. And this means the superhuman. The apprehending of Christ as Lord, the energizing of the will to heed His voice and to go the way of His Cross in heroically bringing His principles to bear on all facts of human life constitute from beginning to end a superhuman undertaking. "The task before us," as the Jerusalem Message proclaims, "is beyond our powers. It can be accomplished only by the Holy Spirit, whose power we receive in its completeness only in the fellowship of Christ's disciples."

IX. THE SUMMONS TO THE HOME BASE

I T HAS BEEN MY OPPORTUNITY TO visit recently all but one of the home-base countries of Christian missions. I wish to share the dominant impressions with reference to the need of strengthening greatly the supporting agencies of this world-wide enterprise. Asia, Africa, and Latin America are not included in this review, although the principles and methods set forth are more or less applicable to the churches of these areas.

My study of the program and problems of the mission boards of Europe, America, and Australasia, and of the churches at their back, convinces me of the imperative need of liberating more largely the all-too-latent lay forces and relating them to the plans of the world mission. Unless I am mistaken, we have in this matter lost ground in recent years. We certainly have not been keeping pace with the widening of our opportunities and with the growing complexity and difficulty of the world-wide spread of Christ's Kingdom. A tremendous loss was suffered when, through the interruption of the World War, the work of the Laymen's Missionary Movement was so largely contracted, and in some fields even disbanded. On both sides of the Atlantic in an incredibly short time it had arrested the attention and enlisted the collaboration of many foremost laymen of the time. It had acquired a prestige and a momentum attended with the largest promise. Notwithstanding commendable and encouraging experiences here and there in individual communities and throughout certain denominations, nothing is to-day beginning to take the place of the impact, the drive, the contagious enthusiasm, and the achieving ability of the old interdenominational and international movement during the first decade of its life.

As I came to close quarters with the missionary societies I was shocked to find in these managing bodies so few laymen under forty years of age. This was true in the United States and in Northern Europe, but more markedly in the British Isles, France, Germany, Canada, Australia, and New Zealand. Then it dawned upon me that in the latter group there was a more significant explanation in the tragic fact of the terrible loss of lives in the war. The men who in those days were from eighteen to thirty years of age would, were they now living, be from thirty to forty-two. Even in these instances this most valid cause but served to double the burden of responsibility which must settle upon the survivors of these younger years in that they must not only furnish their own proper quota of lay workers needed by the Church, but also help fill the gap caused by the sacrificial devotion unto death of so many former comrades.

Why do we need at this time a great accession to the lay forces of the Church of members who will lend themselves to the realization of its missionary objectives?

Certainly we need them in order to develop a dependable financial base for this vast and ever-expanding enterprise. It is noteworthy that solution of nearly all the unsolved problems of Christian missions, including those which as a rule are denominated spiritual, sooner or later involves economic factors. Increasingly, therefore, we must have the participation of laymen. The efficient conduct of this complex, world-wide undertaking demands the business experience, the business judgment, and the business habits, as well as the contacts, access, and influence of laymen, especially those of large affairs. This, admittedly the greatest and most important work in the world, I have found far too often languishing, comparatively inefficient and fruitless because of the lack of their initiative and support.

Then, too, a sense of responsibility and active participation on the part of the laymen themselves are essential in the work of generating confidence and enlisting the coöperation of multitudes among the millions of lay members who are at present totally indifferent to the missionary obligation and challenge. For the develop-

ment of the faith, character, and usefulness of these men
who bear the name of Christ, adequate outlets or opportunities for expression of religious conviction and spirit
are essential.   How true this is of the young men of
to-day.   They need tasks vast, difficult, absorbing, and
tragic to save them from present-day down-grade tendencies, such as growing love of pleasure, ease, extravagance, and softness.

In every land also we must have far more coöperation of laymen in order to Christianize the impact of our
so-called Christian civilization upon the so-called non-
Christian world.   Only as men in business, commerce,
and finance, in the diplomatic and consular service, in
army and navy, in exploration and engineering, in the
many other secular walks of life, and travelers in their
countless social contacts—only as these laymen, by example, by advocacy, and by every other exercise of their
influence, commend and illustrate the Gospel of Christ
can the Christian faith fully permeate modern life.   Such
examples constitute one of the mightiest of all apologetics to followers of non-Christian faiths.

Another reason for augmenting the lay forces of the
missionary movement has in recent years taken on larger
significance than ever: If Christianity through its missionaries and lay representatives is to wage triumphant
warfare abroad, it must not have untaken forts in the
rear—that is, if Christians of Europe, America, and
Australasia are to be of largest helpfulness in Asia and

Africa in the conflict with the opium curse, the drink evil, the traffic in women and children, forced labor or slavery, commercial exploitation and robbery, the cinema at its worst, and a devitalizing materialism or secularism, then it is absolutely necessary that we come to closer and more successful grapple with these and other evils in the so-called Christian West. This can be done only as the lay forces of all Christian churches are called into action.

In the recent laymen's week-end conferences throughout the British Isles, and at luncheons on the Continent and in North America attended by leading laymen, as well as in countless conversations with men of large affairs, I was encouraged to find instant response to such considerations and to the unique challenge offered by the present world situation. I believe the time has come to work out in each country plans which will combine the best features of the pre-war Laymen's Missionary Movement, of current laymen's movements, of some of the most efficient denominational brotherhoods, and of the home-base activities of the foreign departments of the Y. M. C. A. of Anglo-Saxon countries, and the most instructive and fruitful methods employed by the student Christian movements in their service for foreign students. Together with such a development there need to be created a more vivid awareness of the extreme gravity of the present world situation from the Christian standpoint, fresh and more comprehensive plans, a more masterly strategy, and a larger synthesis in the recognition and utilization of constructive forces to be related to the carrying out of Christ's program.   Above all, there must be secured at all costs in each country an abler leadership for this part of the work.   At this very point we shall win or lose.   It is my conviction that right here we have failed.   Not until we recognize that no layman is too important, too busy, or too influential to be called into collaboration and into the exercise of his best powers will the demand of the present creative hour be met.

One of the most encouraging developments of the very recent past has been the initiative taken by groups of prominent laymen of seven denominations in America. After thoroughgoing consideration they have constituted themselves into a joint committee to try to discover and re-state the present-day responsibility of the laymen of their respective communions in relation to the world mission.   To this end they have sent out three representative fact-finding commissions to the three principal fields which these churches are serving.   In the light of the reports of these groups an able commission will during the coming year visit all these fields and make a fresh, detached study of the work.   While aiming always at the ideal, they will seek to discover to what extent existing missionary organizations, policies, and programs should be continued, modified, and supplemented in the formulation of the best practical program for challenging the larger coöperation of laymen to-day.

On every hand there is need of strengthening the financial position of the world mission. In all my visits to mission boards or societies in different parts of the world it has been my practice to allow time for questions and discussion; I do not recall an occasion where in one form or another the financial problem did not emerge. Every board stood in need of more funds. In most instances the work was suffering acutely, and in some was on the threshold of disaster. In a few places, where there was no solicitude with reference to finances, I reached the conclusion that the situation was more alarming than in others where it was regarded as desperate, for this unconcern revealed that the leaders were oblivious to existing awful needs to be met, and to urgent challenges to far larger and more sacrificial help.

Without doubt the Christian cause all over the world is either losing ground, or failing to make triumphant advance, in consequence of failure to press the present unprecedented advantage. It is no time for any organization which bears the name of Christ, with whom resides all power, and which exists primarily for the widening of the limits of His Kingdom, to be satisfied merely with maintaining the *status quo*. As a matter of fact, this cannot be done. There is something startlingly incongruous in any person or community or agency which professes allegiance to the Living Christ—the Fountain

Head of Vitality—who has summoned His followers actually to follow Him, ever being content with a static policy. The beckoning, unerring hand of Christ invariably points to entering open doors and to meeting increasingly the depths of human need. The present is also of all times the most unfitting for a Christian organization to tolerate a deficit—in view of unexampled world-wide opportunities, in view of existing indescribable needs, in view of unmistakable and momentous challenges, in view of the extent of untapped financial resources, and in view of grave dangers resulting from failure to respond.

In no field visited have I been convinced that there need be a deficit, for it has always been admitted that the money needed is in existence. In virtually every Protestant country a disproportionately large part of the wealth is in the hands of the Christians. To a much greater extent than is generally realized Christians are disposed to give money. This is evident from what they are devoting to secular, as well as religious, constructive causes. Careful inquiry reveals that, as a rule, benevolent gifts are not keeping pace with increased income. More surprising is it that in the various denominations from 30 to 70 per cent of the church members are giving nothing to the spread of the Christian religion beyond their own country, although discussions always reveal that among them are numbers as able to give to this cause as are those already on the list of contributors.

When asked to explain why in my judgment so many Christians are not giving generously, if at all, to this vital work, I summarized the matter as follows:

We do not share with possible donors and with those whose gifts are inadequate the up-to-date facts.

We deal too much in generalities and by no means sufficiently with the living and the concrete.

We fail to convey the impression of the greatness of the undertaking.

We present mere fractions in contrast with the wide range and wholeness of the enterprise.

We leave people far too much shut up in narrow denominational, national, and racial compartments rather than ushering them into the large dimensions of the all-inclusive Kingdom of Christ.

We fall short of making real the vital significance and the conscience-shaking requirements of Christ's announced world purpose.

How little we communicate the sense of the splendor, the wonder, the superhuman of it all! "They shall speak of . . . Thy Kingdom, and talk of Thy power."

My contacts with the work before the churches, through world-wide travel and through conversations with administrators of Christian agencies for the spread of the Christian faith, have convinced me that in the years right before us large capital funds will be required if the Christian Church is to be true to her opportunity in non-Christian lands. We cannot begin too soon to prepare to meet these inevitable demands. Much more largely than is being done to-day, we should call to our side outstanding Christian laymen in the realm of finance and bring their large abilities to bear on the formulation and execution of our financial policies. In fact, there are few agencies where it would not be advantageous to secure such help in a complete re-examination and all necessary revision of financial programs and methods. It has been a surprise to discover how few mission boards have on their staffs experts on income production. Where such experts cannot be found they should be developed, and the only way experts are ever developed is by selecting the most likely men for the task and then putting the responsibility on them and backing them to the limit. In recent years, largely as a result of the experience acquired in the war by welfare agencies, such as the Red Cross and the Y. M. C. A., the raising of funds for unselfish causes has been reduced to a science. The Christian movement should avail itself much more largely of this vast and rewarding experience.

The period of financial difficulty and trial through which so many mission and other Christian agencies are passing is not without its advantages, provided the difficulties and trials are regarded as something not to be yielded to, but to be met and overcome. They were de-

signed not as stumblingblocks but as stepping-stones to
larger and richer achievement. Granted this attitude,
the financial problems should lead to the discovery of
new and better ways. That organization is in grave
peril which counts itself as having already attained.
Often the plans and methods of the churches do not
impress discerning men of affairs as embodying the
wisest and most economical use of funds. Such men
do not object to the magnitude of proposed expenditure.
On the contrary, they often wonder at the smallness of
our plans and requirements. But they do emphatically
object to any waste through use of antiquated methods,
or through unnecessary duplication, or otherwise. Such
difficulties at times necessitate and facilitate getting out
of ruts, and, through revision of plans and wise, health-
giving pruning, result in fresh and increased fruitage.
Another marked advantage of a really critical financial
situation is that it may lead to a fresh study of priorities—or putting first things first—to the infinite benefit
of the cause. Financial shortage may and should lead
to greater and better efforts to multiply the number of
givers with resultant enrichment of their lives and widening of the Kingdom. Not least among the benefits of
financial stress is that of increasing the number of money-
raisers, which I sometimes think is the most highly multiplying thing that can be done, next to increasing the
number of intercessors. Chief among the advantages is
that unsolved financial problems, spiritually inter-

preted, may lead to our going Christ's way—the way of the Cross. That invariably means to set gushing the fountains of sacrifice or real self-giving, and that in turn means great harvests, for "except a grain of wheat fall into the ground and die, it abideth by itself alone, but if it die, it beareth [not little but] much fruit."

One of the most disconcerting impressions borne in upon me along the pathway of my journeys was that the youth now thronging the universities and colleges, and likewise those who have graduated from these institutions during the past decade, have by no means been won to the missionary cause. There has been a marked falling off in the number of volunteers for missions, also in the number of undergraduates devoting themselves to the thorough study of missionary questions. The situation is more critical than facts like these imply. Not only do large numbers of students and professors criticize the technique of missions, but there is also on their part a sincere and sharp challenge of some of the most fundamental assumptions—for example, the existence of a personal God, the authority of a moral law, the absolute character of Christian truth. This springs largely from the controlling influence of science and mechanistic scientific conceptions over all thought, and especially in the field of psychology. Thus the total motive and the goal of Christian missions are meaningless to wide ranges of student life. One is not unmindful of exceptions in individual universities here and there. Nor does one overlook the significant fact that students to-day, possibly more largely than ever, are identifying themselves with other forms of altruistic interest and service. Moreover, signs are not wanting in certain parts of the student field, both in North America and in Britain, indicating a turn in the tide. When all of a reassuring character is said which can be said, however, the serious fact remains that this generation, to which are coming heavier burdens than to any preceding generation, must still be won to intelligent and whole-souled allegiance to the world mission of the Christian religion.

While there may not be, and probably will not be, a demand during the next two or three decades for anywhere nearly so many students of the West to become missionaries as during the past two or three decades, there is to-day clamant need of a larger number of the ablest young men and women that the universities can furnish. As I have tried to point out to selected companies of the very flower of the student bodies on both sides of the Atlantic, they are needed to fill important gaps in the missionary ranks. It is solemnizing to see how many posts of major importance are unfilled, and this at the last time when such should be the case. Many more are needed who will put themselves in preparation to provide a worthy succession to faithful workers who, as a result of age and failing strength, must all too soon hand over their great trusts to younger men and women. Others are needed right now to supersede relatively incompetent workers who, with commendable devotion, are holding positions of large importance simply because there are not enough workers of front-line ability and equipment to assume the responsibility. Then, as my journeys in mission fields have shown me in an unforgettable way, there must soon be furnished highly competent reënforcements to avert the breakdown of many a willing and overburdened missionary who is now carrying an impossible load.

On virtually every field there should be additions to the staff in order to make much more highly productive the work of the missionaries already there. I have not visited a hospital, or a Christian college, or a field open to evangelism which I have considered adequately manned. One came away believing that an addition and proper placement, in the near future, of possibly 10 per cent in the number of well-qualified missionaries might well yield 100 per cent increase in results. The growing complexity of the missionary program, calling for higher specialization in function and, therefore, in preparation, necessitates special reënforcements. The reason why in so many fields there are baffling and unsolved problems lies, in part at least, in the want of more new missionaries of the highest qualifications. It is well also to remind ourselves that there are still many totally unoccupied fields, having in them in the aggregate tens of millions of inhabitants, which stand in need of all that we associate with the Christian Gospel. Is there anything, therefore, which has a claim upon the leaders of the Christian forces prior to that of praying, planning, and persevering in well-directed efforts to win for the world program of Christ more young men and women of power of vision, of strength of personality shown in gift of initiative and willingness to accept and discharge responsibility, of capacity to grow and determination to continue to grow all their lives, of willingness to go into training and stay in training longer than their predecessors, of social and ethical passion and concern, of the spirit of adventure and ability to endure hardness, of genuine personal experience of Christ?

Students on both sides of the Atlantic raised with me the question: Granted that we may be needed on the mission field, are we wanted there, especially by the nationals or natives of the country? Before my last round-the-world journey I had discovered that this was one of the most important unanswered questions in the minds of students and, therefore, along the way made it the subject of special inquiry. I was able to bring back the significant report that not in a majority of areas but in them all, including fields occupied by three-quarters of the inhabitants of the non-Christian world, the native Christian leaders without exception authorized me to state that they both need and want more missionaries from the West, but in all instances they speci-

fied that these must be from the ablest and best furnished that the student communities of Europe and
America can provide.

What are the reasons which have militated against
the winning of the new generation to deep conviction in
favor of the world mission and life commitment to it?
The point just mentioned has had its influence. Deeper
still has been a fundamental doubt as to whether Christ
is absolutely essential to the followers of non-Christian
faiths. The widespread spirit and philosophy of secularism has had a benumbing effect. The many and often
worthy opportunities for unselfish service nearer home
or in so-called secular pursuits abroad are deflecting not
a few among the abler youth. The money-making pursuits absorb a vastly disproportionate number. Too
often the advice and pressure of relatives and friends
are exerted in directions quite different from that of
the missionary career. In the main, however, it may
be asserted, in the light of very many contacts with
present-day and former students, that the reason why
more of the ablest are not dedicating themselves to this
greatest work in the world lies in the lack of being exposed to adequate appeals, in inconclusive thinking on
appeals which they have heard or read, and in want of
spirituality.

How meet this basic need? It behooves us to become alarmed, for what calamity could be greater than
to fail at this point—the point of insuring an adequate

leadership of the missionary forces of to-morrow? Then let us act as though we regarded this as the most important single thing we have to do. Without such conviction we shall not pay the price necessary to insure the desired result. With the help of the ablest apologetic writers and speakers we must help youth to answer their fundamental questions pertaining to faith and life. They must be exposed to the most dynamic personalities among the returned missionaries and visiting Christian nationals. The hands of the Student Volunteer Movement, and the Student Christian Movement in general, should be strengthened in every way in our power. In some fields it has been observable that, as a result of uncertainty as to its message, lack of sense of direction and mission as to its objectives, and resultant divided counsels, this movement has ceased to be the world power that it was in earlier years. No sign, therefore, affords more hope for the future than the unmistakable evidences among student movement leaders of honest searchings of heart, humbling confession, and prayerful determination to provide the intellectual and spiritual causes which have invariably been the precursors of every marked advance in the Kingdom of Christ.

None of these great and central elements in the missionary service of the home base can be alert, dynamic, and informed with the needed blend of enthusiasm and skill, apart from an intensive and sustained education of youth, as well as those of more mature years. This generation must intelligently understand both the need of the world and how Christianity meets that need. For this reason we have to press forward with ever-increasing momentum the existing processes of missionary education of boys and girls, of adolescent youth, and of those of more advanced age, and to adapt those processes to the new light that education is receiving to-day from many sources.

The main factors in this work of missionary education must be the leaders in the mission boards and in the local churches, using as tools the mission-study literature provided for every considerable grade of age and of varied educational equipment. The books that are provided every year by the Missionary Education Movement in North America, the United Council for Missionary Education in Britain, and similar bodies in Holland, Scandinavia, Germany, and Australasia are the product of coöperative planning and editing by the educational officers of the mission boards. They are adapted even for parents to read to small children before the reading age, and for each successive age-group up to the layman and the pastor. They are suitable either for reading alone or for group-discussions and for class study. These different grades of literature are used equally in the home, the churches, groups in numerous summer schools and camps, in universities, and in clubs, as well as in the Sunday school and the day school.

This educational movement, nourished by an ever-fresh literature, is of high importance in strengthening what we have seen to be the essential needs of the home base: that is, to supply the churches with convinced lay-men and ministers, to provide the mission boards with a thoroughly informed and genuinely spiritual member-ship, and to create high-grade Student Volunteers from our universities to meet the exacting demands of the mission fields across the world in this momentous day.

X. THE LEADERSHIP FOR THIS
MOMENTOUS DAY

A FRESH STUDY OF THE MEM-
bership of mission boards and their executive staffs,
also of the personnel directing related auxiliary and co-
operative enterprises, convinces one that possibly greater than any other need at the home base, in fact explaining in part why some others are not being more largely
met, is the necessity of strengthening the leadership of
the missionary enterprise. This is particularly necessary in all that pertains to program building, policy
making, determination of priorities, discerning interpretation, and prophetic advocacy. At times I have said
to myself that, if in the plan of God there were forthcoming men and women of really outstanding ability and
equipment for some thirty or forty positions of major
importance in Europe, North America, and Australasia,
such as a few truly creative Christian statesmen among
the present-day leaders of the mission forces, the present overwhelming situation might be adequately met, so

far as this depends upon leaders of the older churches. But the demand for augmenting the directive energy of the undertaking both quantitatively and qualitatively must not be confined to so-called major posts. All along the line higher efficiency is required. The growing complexity and difficulty of the work, the fact that it has entered upon a more advanced and much more exacting stage of development call for reconsideration and restatement of plans and programs in the light of the new outlook in the realms of thought and human relations.

Moreover, account must be taken of the changed psychology of large sections of the supporting constituency of the world program of Christianity both among church members and among those who are outside the churches but who should be interested. This new outlook on life calls for a leadership competent to guide from pulpits, through the printed page, and elsewhere an extensive and continuing educational campaign. For these and other reasons there is certainly demanded a great multiplication in the number and a raising of the qualifications of the leadership in the world mission. Not only the leaders of churches as such are included, but the officers and members of mission boards and of various denominational and interdenominational auxiliary agencies of the boards and of the churches. What should characterize the leadership demanded?

Without doubt we need more leaders who are able to deal in large dimensions. Why? Because the world mission is concerned with the largest unaccomplished work on earth. It embraces every man, woman, and child of every nation and race, in the whole range of individual life and of life's relationships. It involves the greatest issues which can engage the minds of men. It is occupied with the proclamation and application of a great Gospel—a Gospel adequate to satisfy the deepest longings and highest aspirations of the human heart and of the human race. It makes its appeal to the highest and most powerful motives. It must win not only the following of the masses of mankind of all stages of culture, but to this end must also command the attention and enlist the coöperation of men and women of largest affairs, largest influence, and largest possibilities. An outstanding example of truly great leadership was that of Lord Davidson, the late Archbishop of Canterbury. In his rich background of knowledge of the life of the Christian Church through all the centuries, in his altogether exceptional contacts with the work and workers not only of the world-wide Anglican communion but also of other Christian bodies, in his advocacy of an all-inclusive Gospel, and in his keen interest in the great coöperative movements among Christians of different names, he was in a position to exercise an absolutely unique influence in furtherance of the world-wide program of Christ. Soon after he became Archbishop of Canterbury I sought his advice regarding two or three important questions relating to the ecumenical aspect of the work of the World's Student Christian Federation. On that occasion, over twenty-five years ago, he asked that whenever I came to London I should let him know, since he wished to see me. Thenceforth hardly a year passed that I did not have the privilege of visiting him at Lambeth Palace and reporting to him significant developments in the work of the International Missionary Council and the various youth movements to which I was related, and of securing his invaluable counsel on important problems. He always impressed me as having one of the most spacious, truly catholic, and well-informed minds I have ever known; and, to a remarkable degree, he was responsive and coöperative with reference to new visions and plans, especially of the younger generation. One can recall in virtually every communion and every land one or more leaders who within the sphere of their particular calling have manifested like wide vision, wide conceptions, and largeness of soul, and under whose influence the limits of Christ's Kingdom have been extended.

In every country and in every time the leaders who year in and year out achieve the most consistent progress are those who have a vivid and abiding sense of mission—that is, an unshakable conviction that they have been called by God Himself to their work. Their lives are marked by unselfish devotion to an unselfish cause. They invariably give you the impression that the cause is bigger than the man. This has ever been true of the great missionaries, and also of the mission board secretaries and members to whom we trace the great advances. It is this which has imparted contagious power to the lives and messages of Robert P. Wilder and Donald Fraser in their work among students in different parts of the world. Leaders who are under the spell of a divine mission are never discouraged or pessimistic. No matter how many oppose, or how few go with them, they persevere steadfastly in their onward course. They are not deflected by obstacles or by the fears and doubts of others. They go from strength to strength. In times of great confusion or of serious depression and crisis they are the men to whom we turn for the leadership which actually leads out and on.

Sensitiveness to the ordering of Providence is needed in leaders of any great, on-moving cause like that of world-wide missions. It is the quality we associate with the prophet Daniel, of whom it was said he "had understanding of the times." Bishop Walter Lambuth, both in his work as administrator of a great mission board and in performing his functions as bishop, whether working at the home base or engaged in his memorable visits to Asia, Africa, and Latin America, gave constant evidence of his power to recognize the moving, the beckoning hand of his Lord. Any one who has read or heard him describe his experiences when he was sent by his church to discover the right location for a new mission station in the heart of Africa must have been impressed by this fact. The eminent professor of missions, Dr. Gustav Warneck of Germany, who did so much to influence the missionary policy of his day, had rare penetration in discerning times and seasons. I recall how, the last time I had the privilege of visiting him and was outlining my plan of work for the period before me, he suddenly broke out with the remark that I ought to change my program. When I asked him why, he replied, "Instead of making a journey to so many lands as your plan involves, you should at this time of all times go to Japan and spend the whole year there." He then enlarged upon the fact that Japan was the key to the entire Oriental world and that at that moment she was peculiarly open to just such work as we had in view. Subsequent developments made plain how clearly he comprehended the situation.

A mark of the leadership needed in this day, in fact in every time, is that of attentiveness to the voice of God. He has great things to say to all who in true humility will listen to His voice. If we may judge by what He has spoken to the prophets in other days, He may have some very revolutionary things to say to those in our time to whom is entrusted the influencing of the thought and action of His followers. And we may be sure that in a momentous day like this He does not wish us to be contented with simply maintaining the *status quo*. Is it not true that invariably, through Christ and through His followers in every generation, He summons

to press into ever and ever wider ranges of unoccupied
areas of human need? Barth and his school are rendering a much-needed service for this day—that of centering attention on the supreme importance of listening to
the Word of God—to God Himself. All too much we
are prone to listen first, or chiefly, to almost every other
voice—for example, the voice of the latest significant
book, the deliverance of some noted authority, the voice
of the findings of some conference of so-called leading
minds, the voice of some eminent personality of the day,
such as Gandhi—all good in their places, but never to
be assigned the first place. One of the most Christlike,
fruitful workers of the modern centuries, the Reverend
J. Hudson Taylor, the founder of the China Inland Mission, which by the time of his death had a staff of upward of a thousand missionaries scattered over the
provinces of China, was a man who, throughout his entire career administering this vast undertaking, whether
in the British Isles, or the United States, or Canada, or
the continent of Europe, or in China itself, made listening
unto God his constant attitude and unbroken practice. In all my study of the lives and work of Christian
leaders, I have known none more abounding in activity
and more fruitful, but at the same time more stayed on
God as shown in his unruffled poise and peace. The
same might be said of Miss Lilias Trotter, the inspiring
and talented leader of the Algerian Mission Band. Dr.
R. P. Mackay, the wise and greatly beloved leader of

the Canadian Presbyterian Board, was another administrator who literally walked and talked with God, and
the secret of whose abiding influence was the fact that he
so attentively listened for and so faithfully heeded the
voice of the Living God.

A man may be a strategist without being a leader,
but no leader can exert the maximum influence—that is,
render the maximum service—who is not also a good
strategist. Strategy is the science which makes possible
overcoming with relatively small forces far larger forces
which do not have such help. For example, winning for the cause of the world mission a certain influential layman makes possible, it may be, the winning
of scores of other laymen. I recall a recent instance
of this kind, where a member of a mission board,
through enlisting the coöperation of one of the most
prominent laymen in the entire denomination, set in
motion causes which resulted in rallying a score or
more of other leading men of the denomination concerned and those in turn projected a most significant forward movement throughout the denomination. Another
illustration is that of capturing for a cause certain
groups, such as the students, from whose ranks come a
disproportionately large number of leaders in various
walks of life. Then there are means and methods which,
if employed, tremendously facilitate the realization of
missionary objectives—for example, the creation and
intensive training of an inner group of workers, as was

done by Christ. The leader who has discovered how to develop the prayer life of his followers has found a secret of the highest possible augmenting of power. Bishop Thoburn, in his efforts at the home base on behalf of India, proved to be a master strategist in thus utilizing forces. Fletcher S. Brockman, by concentrating on the twenty leading cities of China and upon the modern literati at the most plastic moment in the life of the new China, advanced by a full generation the planting of the Young Men's Christian Association in that land.

A leader for these times must be able to mobilize and wield forces. A strong man can accomplish some things himself, but he can achieve vastly more by multiplying the number who, like himself, will work for his cause. There is so much to do in extending the rule of Christ, and the present forces are so undermanned, that leaders must develop their recruiting and organizing power. This is a voluntary service from beginning to end, and, therefore, the real leader must have the ability to inspire confidence and the resultant following. Moody, the great American evangelist, was more than an evangelist: he was one of the greatest recruiting officers for work at home and abroad that the Christian Church has ever known. Literally hundreds of fruitful missionaries, from the days of the Cambridge Seven down to the last student conference over which he presided at Northfield, owe the fact that they are on the mission field to his challenges to devote their lives to service. His auto-biographical address, *To the Work,* which he delivered so many times with apostolic fervor and conviction, never failed to be the medium through which God delivered His call to men to lose themselves in unselfish causes. Many laymen who for a generation were the great pil-lars in the support of the world mission were led, in his evangelistic meetings, to consecrate their money power and their time to world service. Few institutions on either side of the Atlantic have yielded a greater volume of missionary recruits than the schools at North-field and Mount Hermon and the Moody Institute in Chicago.

Great is the need of a leadership which has the price-less gift of appreciation of youth and sympathy with youth. The men and women with this gift, whether it is exerted from the position of mission board secretary, or of the Christian minister, or teacher, or of the volun-tary lay leader, exercise an influence which reaches into the second and even the third generation. The secret lies in maintaining contacts with youth, identification with their problems, struggles, aspirations, and unselfish purposes, and responsiveness to their visions and plans. William D. Murray, a lawyer of New York City and for over thirty years the chairman of one of the leading foreign boards, has throughout his life devoted all his spare time to serving youth—including the little chil-dren, the preparatory and high-school boys through both

the Young Men's Christian Association and the Boy
Scouts, also the young men of his own country and of
some thirty other lands. Busy as he was, he never let a
year pass without writing a letter in his own hand to the
family of every one of the staff, which expanded during
his administration from a score to over 200. Such identification with youth through a long, full life has not
only kept his own life young and creative but has projected his influence into the years far ahead. Dr. Eu-
gene Stock, the brilliant Editorial Secretary of the
Church Missionary Society, who recently closed his life
of abounding helpfulness at the age of ninety, interested
himself in the Student Christian Movement in its foundation days in Great Britain, America, Australasia, and
the Orient, and right up to the last kept in touch with
developments and helped greatly to hold it true to its
missionary objectives.

The ability to coöperate and determination to co-
operate constitute one of the essential traits of the greatest leaders. The wisest and most effective interdenominational workers are loyal, trusted members of their
own denominations. It should also be emphasized that
at the present stage in the life of the world mission the
leaders who can best meet the demands of the day are
those who believe with deep conviction in both interdenominational and international coöperation, and who
by design take steps to foster it. Dr. J. H. Ritson of the
British and Foreign Bible Society is an ideal illustration,

an honored pillar of great strength in his own denomination, one of the most trusted bridge builders between various communions and also between the Christians of different nations. The whole Church of Christ is also indebted to laymen like the late Dr. Samuel B. Capen, former president of the American Board, and Sir Andrew Fraser of Scotland, and many living laymen on both sides of the Atlantic for their vision and constructive ability in uniting the lay forces in the Laymen's Missionary Movement, which accomplished such a great work, notably during the years preceding the World War.

The gift of humor should not be overlooked, for its possession and use by leaders in this great cause has proved again and again to be of enormous help. It is interesting that most of the outstanding leaders, including some in whom we might not have expected it, reveal a stray vein of this priceless quality. Humor has actually prolonged the life of many a worker overburdened with his serious and exacting tasks. It helps greatly to preserve one's poise, patience, and perspective. And not infrequently has it relieved impossible tension and created an atmosphere in which difficulties were dissipated. What wonderful triumphs of this unconscious art have not been achieved on critical occasions in gatherings for shaping missionary policy, by men like Silas McBee, editor of *The Constructive Quarterly*, Dr. Wardlaw Thompson, of the London Missionary Society, one of the ablest missionary statesmen of mod-

ern times, Alfred E. Marling, formerly president of the
New York Chamber of Commerce, and Dr. James Endicott, the brilliant executive head of the missionary society of the United Church of Canada; in fact the list
might run on indefinitely.

The leaders in momentous days like these must be able
to feed on difficulties. Probably never has there been
a time in the history of the expansion of the Christian
religion when the leaders at the home base, in fact in
every country, were confronted with such a concentration of unsolved problems and impossible difficulties.
We have all too many among them who have become
expert in seeing lions in the path, men who have become habituated to taking counsel with their fears.
Great is the need of more men and women in positions
of leadership who, while not failing to see with clear
and steady gaze all the adverse or opposing facts and
factors, are even more determined to take counsel with
their faith. In reality is not this one of the chief functions
of a leader? The true leader is at his best under most
baffling circumstances. The board secretaries and board
members to whom the churches are most indebted are
not those associated with so-called strategic retreats but
with steady, triumphant progress under conditions where
the majority insisted that advance was impossible. If
any one at the home base is ever tempted to fall down or
give up in front of difficulties let him turn afresh to the
biographies of Adoniram Judson of Burma, William

Carey of India, Joseph Neesima of Japan, and Aggrey of Africa, and see how, in the face of obstacles and opposition the like of which we do not know, they turned apparent defeats into immortal triumphs.

To sum up the requirements of the leadership of this momentous day, the demand is for men and women who can furnish a real lead. The reason for this is convincing: the world mission at Jerusalem unmistakably entered upon a new epoch, and this demands a new orientation to the missionary task. This calls for leadership possessing not only insight into the conditions, trends, and needs of the present but also foresight or prophetic vision of things to come. It also demands leaders with decision of character who can think conclusively and act in the light of the facts. They must have the spirit of adventure, courage, and unselfish abandon. Theirs must be the contagious optimism resting on the great basic facts and assumptions of the Christian faith. No pessimist ever rose to the heights of great leadership. One must himself lead off, if others are to follow. Faith is literally the victory that overcomes the world.

There is nothing which is quite so much needed throughout the world-wide mission of the Christian religion as a fresh summons to the impossible. For is this not precisely what Christ gave when He launched His world-wide program? Can those of us who are called upon to lead forward His world mission do less? Those who regard or treat Christian missions as less than an adventure in the realm of the humanly impossible must entertain superficial views as to the reality of the difficulties or unworthy views as to the superhuman source and resources of the undertaking. It is urgently desirable that we come to see and then afford fresh demonstrations of the fact that in the sublime enterprise of making Christ known, loved, obeyed, and exemplified in life and human relationships it is easier to accomplish very great, bafflingly difficult, even impossible things than the easy, the simple, and the possible. Why is this so?

For one reason, the overwhelming and the humanly-speaking impossible makes the great appeal to the imagination, the faculty of all our faculties which is least exercised.

It requires such adventure, likewise, to call out our other latent powers. How comparatively latent are the energies of mind, heart, and will of Christians in these days!

It takes a program such as world-wide missions, properly conceived and presented in all their massive greatness, wholeness, oneness, and revolutionary and transforming power, to arrest the attention and command the coöperation of men and women of large affairs and of the greatest power and influence.

It is my deep belief that here also lies one of the secrets of winning to the mission cause the new generation. To them there is nothing like the attraction of hard things. Here also is the secret of victory. Church history has taught no lesson more eloquently than that where the spread of the Gospel is difficult heroic faith has made it triumphant.

But the governing reason, which becomes the abso-lutely convincing reason, why it is easier to achieve the impossible is the fact that in the pathway of this quest and of the realization of the objectives of the world mission we find ourselves not alone but in the Divine Presence and in the pathway of an ever-deepening acquaintance with God and an ever-enlarging experience of His creative, life-giving power.

It was to this overwhelming conviction that the leaders assembled at Jerusalem were driven by the irresistible logic of the facts of human need across the world, which we have now all too swiftly surveyed, when considered in the light of the Good News in Christ. As the Message said in its culminating and final words:

"We are persuaded that we and all Christian people must seek a more heroic practice of the Gospel. It cannot be that our present complacency and moderation are a faithful expression of the mind of Christ, and of the meaning of His Cross and Resurrection in the midst of the wrong and want and sin of our modern world. As we contemplate the work with which Christ has charged His Church, we who are met here on the Mount of Olives, in sight of Calvary, would take up for ourselves and summon those from whom we come and to whom we return to take up with us the Cross of Christ, and all that for which it stands, and to go forth into the world to live in the fellowship of His sufferings and by the power of

His resurrection, in hope and expectation of His glorious Kingdom." [1]

[1] *The Christian Life and Message in Relation to Non-Christian Systems of Thought and Life.* The Jerusalem Meeting of the International Missionary Council, March 24–April 8, 1928, Vol. I, pp. 413 f. (New York: The International Missionary Council, 1928). Copyright. Used by permission.

APPENDIX

The Christian Message

(A Statement adopted by the International Missionary Council at Jerusalem, March 24–April 8, 1928)

GO AND MAKE DISCIPLES OF ALL NATIONS

THROUGHOUT the world there is a sense of insecurity and instability. Ancient religions are undergoing modification, and in some regions dissolution, as scientific and commercial development alter the current of men's thought. Institutions regarded with age-long veneration are discarded or called in question; well-established standards of moral conduct are brought under criticism; and countries called Christian feel the stress as truly as the peoples of Asia and Africa. On all sides doubt is expressed whether there is any absolute truth or goodness. A new relativism struggles to enthrone itself in human thought.

Along with this is found the existence of world-wide suffering and pain, which expresses itself partly in a despair of all higher values, partly in a tragically earnest quest of a new basis for life and thought, in the birthpangs of rising nationalism, in the ever-keener consciousness of race- and class-oppression.

Amid widespread indifference and immersion in material concerns we also find everywhere, now in noble forms and now in license or extravagance, a great yearning, especially among the youth of the world, for the full and untrammeled expression of personality, for spiritual leadership and author-

249

ity, for reality in religion, for social justice, for human brotherhood, for international peace.

In this world, bewildered and groping for its way, Jesus Christ has drawn to Himself the attention and admiration of mankind as never before. He stands before men as plainly greater than Western civilization, greater than the Christianity that the world has come to know. Many who have not hitherto been won to His Church yet find in Him their hero and their ideal. Within His Church there is a widespread desire for unity centered in His Person.

OUR MESSAGE

Against this background and in relation to it, we have to proclaim our message.

Our message is Jesus Christ. He is the revelation of what God is and of what man through Him may become. In Him we come face to face with the Ultimate Reality of the universe; He makes known to us God as our Father, perfect and infinite in love and in righteousness; for in Him we find God incarnate, the final, yet ever-unfolding, revelation of the God in whom we live and move and have our being.

We hold that through all that happens, in light and in darkness, God is working, ruling and overruling. Jesus Christ, in His life and through His death and resurrection, has disclosed to us the Father, the Supreme Reality, as almighty Love, reconciling the world to Himself by the Cross, suffering with men in their struggle against sin and evil, bearing with them and for them the burden of sin, forgiving them as they, with forgiveness in their own hearts, turn to Him in repentance and faith, and creating humanity anew for an ever-growing, ever-enlarging, everlasting life.

The vision of God in Christ brings and deepens the sense

of sin and guilt. We are not worthy of His love; we have by
our own fault opposed His holy will. Yet that same vision
which brings the sense of guilt brings also the assurance of
pardon, if only we yield ourselves in faith to the spirit of
Christ so that His redeeming love may avail to reconcile us
to God.

We reaffirm that God, as Jesus Christ has revealed Him,
requires all His children, in all circumstances, at all times, and
in all human relationships, to live in love and righteousness
for His glory. By the resurrection of Christ and the gift of
the Holy Spirit God offers His own power to men that they
may be fellow workers with Him, and urges them on to a life
of adventure and self-sacrifice in preparation for the coming
of His Kingdom in its fullness.

We will not ourselves offer any further formulation of the
Christian message, for we remember that as lately as in
August, 1927, the World Conference on Faith and Order met
at Lausanne, and that a statement on this subject was issued
from that conference after it had been received with full acceptance. We are glad to make this our own.

"The message of the Church to the world is and must always
remain the Gospel of Jesus Christ.

"The Gospel is the joyful message of redemption, both here
and hereafter, the gift of God to sinful man in Jesus Christ.

"The world was prepared for the coming of Christ through
the activities of God's Holy Spirit in all humanity, but especially in His revelation as given in the Old Testament; and
in the fullness of time the eternal Word of God became incarnate and was made man, Jesus Christ, the Son of God and the
Son of Man, full of grace and truth.

"Through His life and teaching, His call to repentance, His
proclamation of the coming of the Kingdom of God and of

judgment, His suffering and death, His resurrection and exaltation to the right hand of the Father, and by the mission of the Holy Spirit, He has brought to us forgiveness of sins, and has revealed the fullness of the living God and His boundless love toward us. By the appeal of that love, shown in its completeness on the Cross, He summons us to the new life of faith, self-sacrifice, and devotion to His service and the service of men.

"Jesus Christ, as the crucified and the living One, as Saviour and Lord, is also the center of the world-wide Gospel of the Apostles and the Church. Because He Himself is the Gospel, the Gospel is the message of the Church to the world. It is more than a philosophical theory; more than a theological system; more than a program for material betterment. The Gospel is rather the gift of a new world from God to this old world of sin and death; still more, it is the victory over sin and death, the revelation of eternal life in Him who has knit together the whole family in heaven and on earth in the communion of saints, united in the fellowship of service, of prayer, and of praise.

"The Gospel is the prophetic call to sinful man to turn to God, the joyful tidings of justification and of sanctification to those who believe in Christ. It is the comfort of those who suffer; to those who are bound it is the assurance of the glorious liberty of the sons of God. The Gospel brings peace and joy to the heart, and produces in men self-denial, readiness for brotherly service, and compassionate love. It offers the supreme goal for the aspirations of youth, strength to the toiler, rest to the weary, and the crown of life to the martyr.

"The Gospel is the sure source of power for social regeneration. It proclaims the only way by which humanity can escape from those class- and race-hatreds which devastate society at present into the enjoyment of national well-being and international friendship and peace. It is also a gracious invitation to the non-Christian world, East and West, to enter into the joy of the living Lord.

"Sympathizing with the anguish of our generation, with its longing for intellectual sincerity, social justice, and spiritual inspiration, the Church in the eternal Gospel meets the needs and fulfills the God-given aspirations of the modern world. Consequently, as in the past so also in the present, the Gospel is the only way of salvation. Thus, through His Church, the living Christ still says to men, 'Come unto me! . . . He that followeth me shall not walk in darkness, but shall have the light of life.' "

THE MISSIONARY MOTIVE

If such is our message, the motive for its delivery should be plain. The Gospel is the answer to the world's greatest need. It is not our discovery or achievement; it rests on what we recognize as an act of God. It is first and foremost "Good News." It announces glorious Truth. Its very nature forbids us to say that it may be the right belief for some but not for others. Either it is true for all, or it is not true at all.

But questions concerning the missionary motive have been widely raised, and such a change in the habits of men's thoughts as the last generation has witnessed must call for a reëxamination of these questions.

Accordingly we would lay bare the motives that impel us to the missionary enterprise. We recognize that the health of our movement and of our souls demands a self-criticism that is relentless and exacting.

In searching for the motives that impel us we find ourselves eliminating decisively and at once certain motives that may seem, in the minds of some, to have become mixed up with purer motives in the history of the movement. We repudiate any attempt on the part of trade or of governments, openly or covertly, to use the missionary cause for ulterior purposes. Our Gospel by its very nature and by its declaration of the sacredness of human personality stands against all exploitation of man by man, so that we cannot tolerate any desire, conscious or unconscious, to use this movement for purposes of fastening a bondage, economic, political, or social, on any people.

Going deeper, on our part we would repudiate any symptoms of a religious imperialism that would desire to impose beliefs and practices on others in order to manage their souls in their supposed interests. We obey a God who respects our wills and we desire to respect those of others.

Nor have we the desire to bind up our Gospel with fixed ecclesiastical forms which derive their meaning from the experience of the Western Church. Rather the aim should be to place at the disposal of the younger churches of all lands our collective and historical experience. We believe that much of that heritage has come out of reality and will be worth sharing. But we ardently desire that the younger churches should express the Gospel through their own genius and through forms suitable to their racial heritage. There must be no desire to lord it over the personal or collective faith of others.

Our true and compelling motive lies in the very nature of the God to whom we have given our hearts. Since He is love, His very nature is to share. Christ is the expression in time of the eternal self-giving of the Father. Coming into fellowship with Christ we find in ourselves an overmastering impulse to share Him with others. We are constrained by the love of

Christ and by obedience to His last command. He Himself said, "I am come that they might have life, and that they might have it more abundantly," and our experience corroborates it. He has become life to us. We would share that life.

We are assured that Christ comes with an offer of life to man and to societies and to nations. We believe that in Him the shackles of moral evil and guilt are broken from human personality and that men are made free, and that such personal freedom lies at the basis of the freeing of society from cramping custom and blighting social practices and political bondage, so that in Christ men and societies and nations may stand up free and complete.

We find in Christ, and especially in His Cross and Resurrection, an inexhaustible source of power that makes us hope when there is no hope. We believe that through it men and societies and nations that have lost their moral nerve to live will be quickened into life.

We have a pattern in our minds as to what form that life should take. We believe in a Christlike world. We know nothing better; we can be content with nothing less. We do not go to the nations called non-Christian because they are the worst of the world and they alone are in need; we go because they are a part of the world and share with us in the same human need—the need of redemption from ourselves and from sin, the need to have life complete and abundant and to be remade after this pattern of Christlikeness. We desire a world in which Christ will not be crucified but where His Spirit shall reign.

We believe that men are made for Christ and cannot really live apart from Him. Our fathers were impressed with the horror that men should die without Christ—we share that horror; we are impressed also with the horror that men should live without Christ.

Herein lies the Christian motive; it is simple. We cannot live without Christ and we cannot bear to think of men living without Him. We cannot be content to live in a world that is un-Christlike. We cannot be idle while the yearning of His heart for His brethren is unsatisfied.

Since Christ is the motive, the end of Christian missions fits in with that motive. Its end is nothing less than the production of Christlike character in individuals and societies and nations through faith in and fellowship with Christ the living Saviour, and through corporate sharing of life in a divine society.

Christ is our motive and Christ is our end. We must give nothing less, and we can give nothing more.

THE SPIRIT OF OUR ENDEAVOR

Our approach to our task must be made in humility and penitence and love: in humility, because it is not our own message which we bring, but God's, and if in our delivery of it self-assertion finds any place we shall spoil that message and hinder its acceptance; in penitence because our fathers and we ourselves have been so blind to many of the implications of our faith; in love, because our message is the Gospel of the Love of God, and only by love in our own hearts for those to whom we speak can we make known its power or its true nature.

Especially do we confess the sluggishness of the older churches to realize and discharge their responsibility to carry the Gospel to all the world; and all alike we confess our neglect to bring the ordering of men's lives into conformity with the spirit of Christ. The Church has not firmly and effectively set its face against race-hatred, race-envy, race-contempt, or against social envy and contempt and class-bitterness, or against racial, national, and social pride, or against the lust for wealth and exploitation of the poor or weak. We believe that the Gospel "proclaims the only way by which humanity can escape from class- and race-hatred." But we are forced to recognize that such a claim requires to be made good and that the record of Christendom hitherto is not sufficient to sustain it. Nor has it sufficiently sought out the good and noble elements in the non-Christian beliefs, that it might learn that deeper personal fellowship with adherents of those beliefs wherein they may be more powerfully drawn to the living Christ. We know that, even apart from conscious knowledge of Him, when men are true to the best light they have, they are able to effect some real deliverance from many of the evils that afflict the world; and this should prompt us the more to help them to find the fullness of light and power in Christ.

But while we record these failures we are also bound to record with thankfulness the achievements of the Christian Church in this field. The difference between the Europe known to St. Paul and the Europe known to Dante, to Luther, to Wesley is plain for all to see. From every quarter of the globe comes testimony to the liberation effected by Christ for women. Since the vast changes made by the development of industrialism have come to be appreciated, every country has had its Christian social movements and the Universal Conference on Life and Work, held at Stockholm in 1925, revealed how widespread and influential these have become. Truly our efforts have not been commensurate with the needs of the world or with the claim of Christ; but in what has been accomplished and attempted we have already great encouragement for the days to come. In particular there is a growing sensitiveness of conscience with regard to war and the conditions that may lead up to it. For all these indications of the growing power of the spirit of Christ among Christians we thank God. And we call on all Christian people to be ready for pioneering thought and action in the name of Christ. Too often the Church has adopted new truth, or new goals for enterprise, only when the danger attached to them is over. There is a risk of rashness; but there is also possible an excessive caution by which, because His Church hangs back, the glory of new truth or enterprise which rightly belongs to Christ is in men's thoughts denied to Him.

THE CALL TO THE WORLD

Filled with conviction that Jesus Christ is indeed the Saviour of the world, and conscious of a desperate need in ourselves and in all the world for what He only can supply, we call upon our fellow Christians and all our fellow men to turn again to Him for pardon and for power.

1. To all the Churches of Christ we call: that they stand firmly upon the rock of Christian conviction and wholeheartedly accept its missionary obligations; that they go forward in full loyalty to Christ to discover and to express, in the power and freedom of the Holy Spirit, the treasures in His unsearchable riches which it is the privilege and duty of each to win for the Universal Church; that they strive to deliver the name of Christ and of Christianity from complicity in any evil or injustice.

Those who proclaim Christ's message must give evidence for it in their own lives and in the social institutions which they uphold. It is by living Christ among men that we may most effectively lift Him up before them. The spirit that returns love for hate, and overcomes evil with good, must be evidently present in those who would be witnesses for Christ. They are also bound to exert all their influence to secure that the social, international, and interracial relationships in the midst of which their work is done be subordinate to and expressive of His Spirit. Especially must it be a serious obstacle to missionary effort if a non-Christian country feels that the relation of the so-called Christian countries to itself is morally unsound or is alien from the principles of Christ, and the Church must be ready for labor and sacrifice to remove whatever is justly so condemned.

The task before us is beyond our powers. It can be accomplished only by the Holy Spirit, whose power we receive in its completeness only in the fellowship of Christ's disciples. We call all followers of Christ to take their full share as members of His Body, which is the Church; no discontent with its organization or tradition or failings should be allowed to keep us outside its fold; the isolated Christian is impoverished in his spiritual life and impotent in his activities; our strength, both inward and outward, is in the living fellowship. But in these hurried and feverish days there is also more need than ever for the deepening of our spiritual life through periodical detachment from the world and its need in lonely communion with God. We desire also to call for a greater volume of intercessory prayer. The whole Church should be earnest and instant in prayer, each part for every other, and all together for the Church's unity and for the hallowing of God's Name throughout the world.

Further, we call on Christians in all lands who are trained in science, art, or philosophy to devote their talents to the working out of that Christian view of life and the world which we sorely need to secure us against instability, bewilderment, and extravagance.

Lastly, we urge that every possible step be taken to make real the fellowship of the Gospel. The churches of the West send missions and missions-of-help to the churches of Africa and Asia. We believe that the time is come when all would gain if the younger churches were invited to send missions-of-help to the churches of Europe and America, that they may minister of their treasure to the spiritual life of those to whom they come.

2. To non-Christians also we make our call. We rejoice to think that just because in Jesus Christ the light that lighteneth every man shone forth in its full splendor, we find rays of that same light where He is unknown or even is rejected. We welcome every noble quality in non-Christian persons or systems as further proof that the Father, who sent His Son into the world, has nowhere left Himself without witness.

Thus, merely to give illustration, and making no attempt to estimate the spiritual value of other religions to their adherents, we recognize as part of the one Truth that sense of the Majesty of God and the consequent reverence in worship, which are conspicuous in Islam; the deep sympathy for the world's sorrow and unselfish search for the way of escape, which are at the heart of Buddhism; the desire for contact with Ultimate Reality conceived as spiritual, which is prominent in Hinduism; the belief in a moral order of the universe and consequent insistence on moral conduct, which are inculcated by Confucianism; the disinterested pursuit of truth and of human welfare which are often found in those who stand for secular civilization but do not accept Christ as their Lord and Saviour.

Especially we make our call to the Jewish people, whose

Scriptures have become our own, and "of whom is Christ as concerning the flesh," that with open heart they turn to that Lord in whom is fulfilled the hope of their nation, its prophetic message, and its zeal for holiness. And we call upon our fellow Christians in all lands to show to Jews that loving-kindness that has too seldom been shown towards them.

We call on the followers of non-Christian religions to join with us in the study of Jesus Christ as He stands before us in the Scriptures, His place in the life of the world, and His power to satisfy the human heart; to hold fast to faith in the unseen and eternal in face of the growing materialism of the world; to coöperate with us against all the evils of secularism; to respect freedom of conscience so that men may confess Christ without separation from home and friends; and to discern that all the good of which men have conceived is fulfilled and secured in Christ.

Christianity is not a Western religion, nor is it yet effectively accepted by the Western world as a whole. Christ belongs to the peoples of Africa and Asia as much as to the European or American. We call all men to equal fellowship in Him. But to come to Him is always self-surrender. We must not come in the pride of national heritage or religious tradition; he who would enter the Kingdom of God must become as a little child, though in that Kingdom are all the treasures of man's aspirations, consecrated and harmonized. Just because Christ is the self-disclosure of the One God, all human aspirations are toward Him, and yet of no human tradition is He merely the continuation. He is the desire of all nations; but he is always more, and other, than they had desired before they learned of Him.

But we would insist that when the Gospel of the Love of God comes home with power to the human heart, it speaks to each man, not as Moslem or as Buddhist, or as an adherent of any system, but just as man. And while we rightly study other religions in order to approach men wisely, yet at the last we speak as men to men, inviting them to share with us the pardon and the life that we have found in Christ.

3. To all who inherit the benefits of secular civilization and contribute to its advancement we make our call. We claim for Christ the labors of scientists and artists. We recognize their service to His cause in dispersing the darkness of ignorance, superstition, and vulgarity. We appreciate also the noble elements that are found in nationalist movements and in patriotism, the loyalty, the self-devotion, the idealism, which love of country can inspire. But even these may lead to strife and bitterness and narrowness of outlook if they are not dedicated to Christ; in His universal Kingdom of Love all nations by right are provinces and fulfill their own true destiny only in His service. When patriotism and science are not consecrated they are often debased into self-assertion, exploitation, and the service of greed. Indeed, throughout all nations the great peril of our time arises from that immense development of man's power over the resources of nature which has been the great characteristic of our epoch. This power gives opportunity for wealth of interest, and, through facilities of communication, for freedom of intercourse such as has never been known. But it has outgrown our spiritual and moral control.

Amid the clashes of industrial strife the Gospel summons men to work together as brothers in providing for the human family the economic basis of the good life. In the presence of social antipathies and exclusiveness the Gospel insists that we are members of one family, and that our Father desires for each a full and equal opportunity to attain to His own complete development, and to make his special contribution to the richness of the family life. Confronted by international relations that constantly flout Christ's law of love, there is laid on all who bear His name the solemn obligation to labor unceasingly for a new world-order in which justice shall be secured for all peoples, and every occasion for war or threat of war be removed.

Such changes can be brought about only through an unreserved acceptance of Christ's way of love, and by the courageous and sacrificial living that it demands. Still ringing in our ears is the call, "Be not conformed to this world: but be ye transformed by the renewing of your mind."

CONCLUSION

In our conference together we have seen more clearly the fullness and sufficiency of the Gospel and our own need of the salvation of Christ. The enlarging thoughts of the generation find the Gospel and the Saviour ever richer and greater than men had known.

This deepened assurance of the adequacy and universality of the Gospel, however, is not enough. More effective ways must be found for its proclamation, not to systems of opinion only, but to human beings, to men and women for whom Christ died. The most thorough and convincing intellectual statement of Christianity is necessary, but such statements cannot suffice. The Gospel must be expressed also in simplicity and love, and offered to men's hearts and minds by word and deed and life, by righteousness and loving-kindness, by justice, sympathy, and compassion, by ministry to human needs and to the deep want of the world.

As together, Christians of all lands, we have surveyed the world and the needs of men, we are convinced of the urgent necessity for a great increase in the Christian forces in all

countries, and for a still fuller measure of coöperation between the churches of all nations in more speedily laying the
claim of Christ upon all the unoccupied areas of the world
and of human life.

We are persuaded that we and all Christian people must
seek a more heroic practice of the Gospel. It cannot be that
our present complacency and moderation are a faithful expression of the mind of Christ, and of the meaning of His
Cross and Resurrection in the midst of the wrong and want and
sin of our modern world. As we contemplate the work with
which Christ has charged His Church, we who are met here
on the Mount of Olives, in sight of Calvary, would take up
for ourselves and summon those from whom we come and to
whom we return to take up with us the Cross of Christ, and
all that for which it stands, and to go forth into the world
to live in the fellowship of His sufferings and by the power of
His resurrection, in hope and expectation of His glorious
Kingdom.

BIBLIOGRAPHY

Periodicals and Conference Proceedings

1. Periodicals

The Chinese Recorder, Journal of the Christian Movement in China. Shanghai: 1910 to date.

The Church Overseas. London: Issued for the Missionary Council of the Church Assembly by the Press Publications Board, 1928 to date; also *The Church Missionary Review,* 1910–1927, and *The East and the West,* 1910–1927.

Foreign Affairs, an American Quarterly Review. New York: Council on Foreign Relations, Inc., 1923 to date.

The International Review of Missions. London and New York: International Missionary Council, 1912 to date.

The Japan Christian Quarterly; before 1926 *The Japan Evangelist.* Tokyo: The Christian Literature Society of Japan, 1910 to date.

The Moslem World. New York: Missionary Review Publishing Company, 1911 to date.

The National Christian Council Review; before 1924 *The Harvest Field.* Organ of the National Christian Council of India, Burma, and Ceylon. Mysore City: 1910 to date.

Neue Allgemeine Missionszeitschrift; before 1923 *Allgemeine Missionszeitschrift.* Gütersloh: Bertelsmann, 1910 to date.

The Round Table, a Quarterly Review of the Politics of the British Commonwealth. London: Macmillan, 1910 to date.

The South African Outlook, a Journal dealing with Native Problems, Missionary News, and Social Service. Lovedale: Lovedale Press, 1922 to date.

Zeitschrift für Missionswissenschaft und Religionswissenschaft.
Münster in Westfalen: Aschendorffsche Verlagsbuchhand-
lung, 1911 to date.

2. Conference Proceedings

AFRICA. *The Christian Mission in Africa: A Study Based on
the Work of the International Conference at Le Zoute, Bel-
gium, September 14–21, 1926,* by Edwin W. Smith. New
York: International Missionary Council, 1926.

BREMEN. *Verhandlungen der Kontinentalen Missionskonferen-
zen in Bremen.* Bremen: Kommissionsverlag der Norddeutschen Missions-Gesellschaft, 1913 to date.

CHINESE CHURCH. *The Chinese Church as Revealed in the
National Christian Conference held in Shanghai, May 2–11,
1922,* edited by F. Rawlinson, Helen Thoburn, and D. Mac-
Gillivray. Shanghai: The Oriental Press.

CONGO. *Message of the Congo Jubilee and West Africa Conference, Leopoldville, Congo Belge* [September 15–23,
1928], by Dr. and Mrs. Henri Anet. Leopoldville: Conseil
Protestant du Congo, 1929.

CONTINUATION COMMITTEE. *The Continuation Committee Conferences in Asia, 1912-1913. A Brief Account of the Conferences, together with their Findings and Lists of Members.*
New York: Published by the Chairman of the Continuation
Committee, 1913.

C. O. P. E. C. *Conference on Christian Politics, Economics,
and Citizenship; the Proceedings of C. O. P. E. C.* London, New York, etc.: Published for the Conference Committee by Longmans, 1924. 12 vol.

EDINBURGH. World Missionary Conference, Edinburgh, 1910,
Report of Commissions I-VIII. New York: Revell, 1910.
9 vol.

Echoes from Edinburgh, 1910; an Account and Interpretation of the World Missionary Conference, by W. H. T. Gairdner. New York: Revell, 1910.

GREAT BRITAIN AND IRELAND. Conference of Missionary Societies in Great Britain and Ireland, *Reports of Annual Conferences.* London: Edinburgh House, 1911 to date.

JERUSALEM. *The Jerusalem Meeting of the International Missionary Council, March 24–April 8, 1928.* New York: International Missionary Council, 1928. 8 vol.

Roads to the City of God, by Basil Mathews. Garden City: Doubleday, Doran, 1928.

JEWS. *The Christian Approach to the Jew: . . . A Report of Conferences . . . held at Budapest and Warsaw in April, 1927.* London: Edinburgh House, 1927.

Christians and Jews: A Report of the Atlantic City Conference on the Christian Approach to the Jews, May 12–15, 1931. New York: International Missionary Council, 1931.

LATIN AMERICA. *Christian Work in Latin America. . . . Being the Reports of Commissions I-VIII. . . . Presented to the Congress on Christian Work in Latin America, Panama, February, 1916.* New York: Missionary Education Movement, 1916–17. 3 vol.

Christian Work in South America: Official Report of the Congress on Christian Work in South America, Montevideo, Uruguay, April, 1925, edited by Robert E. Speer, Samuel G. Inman, and Frank K. Sanders. New York: Revell, 1925. 2 vol.

Evangelicals at Havana: Being an Account of the Hispanic American Evangelical Congress at Havana, Cuba, June 20-30, 1929, by Samuel Guy Inman. New York: Committee on Coöperation in Latin America.

LAUSANNE. *Faith and Order: Proceedings of the World Conference, Lausanne, August 3–21, 1927*, edited by H. N. Bate. London: Student Christian Movement, 1927.

Lausanne 1927: An Interpretation of the World Conference on Faith and Order Held at Lausanne, August 3–21, 1927, by Edward S. Woods; with an Introduction by His Grace the Archbishop of Canterbury. London: Student Christian Movement, 1927.

MOSLEMS. *Conferences of Christian Workers Among Moslems, 1924.* New York: International Missionary Council, 1924.

NORTH AMERICA. The Foreign Missions Conference of North America, *Reports of Annual Meetings of the Conference of Foreign Mission Boards in Canada and in the United States.* New York: 1910 to date.

PACIFIC RELATIONS. *Institute of Pacific Relations, Honolulu, 1925, History, Organization, Proceedings, Discussions, and Addresses.* Honolulu: Published by the Institute, 1925.

Problems of the Pacific: Proceedings of the Second Conference of the Institute of Pacific Relations, Honolulu, Hawaii, July 15-29, 1927, edited by J. B. Condliffe. Chicago: University of Chicago Press, 1928.

Problems of the Pacific, 1929: Proceedings of the Third Conference of the Institute of Pacific Relations, Nara and Kyoto, Japan, 1929, edited by J. B. Condliffe. Chicago: University of Chicago Press, 1930.

STOCKHOLM. *Universal Christian Conference on Life and Work, Stockholm, 1925*, edited by G. K. A. Bell. The Stockholm Conference, 1925; the Official Report of the Universal Christian Conference on Life and Work, . . . August 19–30, 1925. London: Oxford University Press, 1926.

Chapter I

General

Allen, G. C., *Modern Japan and Its Problems*. London: Allen & Unwin, 1928.

Armstrong, Harold, *Turkey and Syria Reborn*. London: Lane, 1930.

Blakeslee, George H., *The Pacific Area: An International Survey*. Boston: World Peace Foundation, 1929. (Pam.)

Buell, Raymond Leslie, *The Native Problem in Africa*. New York: Macmillan, 1928. 2 vol.

Corey, Stephen J., *The Preacher and His Missionary Message*. Nashville: Cokesbury, 1930.

Foster, John, *Chinese Realities*. London: Edinburgh House, 1928.

Gibbons, Herbert A., *The New Map of South America*. New York: Century, 1928.

High, Stanley, *A Waking World*. New York: Abingdon, 1928.

Holcombe, Arthur N., *The Spirit of the Chinese Revolution*. The Lowell Institute Lectures. New York: Knopf, 1930.

Macnicol, Nicol, *India in the Dark Wood*. London: Livingstone, 1930.

Paton, William, *A Faith for the World*. Edinburgh: Turnbull and Spears, 1929.

Paul, K. T., *The British Connection with India*. London: Student Christian Movement, 1928.

Peffer, Nathaniel, *China: The Collapse of a Civilization*. New York: Day, 1930.

Phillips, Ray E., *The Bantu Are Coming: Phases of South Africa's Race Problem*. London: Student Christian Movement, 1930.

RADHAKRISHNAN, S., *Kalki, or the Future of Civilization.* London: Kegan Paul, 1929.

RIPPY, J. FRED, *Latin America in World Politics.* New York: Knopf, 1928.

"A Survey of the Year 1930" (in *The International Review of Missions,* Volume XX, No. 77; London and New York, January, 1931).

"Tendencies, Trends, and Opportunities" (in *Evangelical Christianity in the Philippines,* by Camilo Osias and Avelina Lorenzana). Dayton Ohio: United Brethren Publishing House, 1931. Chapter XII.

THOMPSON, EDWARD, *The Reconstruction of India.* London: Faber, 1930.

TSURUMI, YUSUKE, *Present-Day Japan.* New York: Columbia University Press, 1926.

TYAU, MIN-CH'IEN T. Z., Editor, *Two Years of Nationalist China.* Shanghai: Kelly and Walsh, 1930.

WOOLACOTT, J. E., *India on Trial: A Study of Present Conditions.* London: Macmillan, 1929.

WORCESTER, DEAN C., and RALSTON HAYDEN, *The Philippines, Past and Present.* New York: Macmillan, 1930.

YOUNGHUSBAND, SIR FRANCIS, *Dawn in India: British Purpose and Indian Aspiration.* London: Murray, 1930.

Nationalism

BARKER, ERNEST, *National Character and the Factors in Its Formation.* London: Methuen, 1927.

CLOSE, UPTON, *The Revolt of Asia.* New York: Putnam's, 1927.

HAYES, CARLTON JOSEPH HUNTLEY, *Essays on Nationalism.* New York: Macmillan, 1926.

KOHN, HANS, *A History of Nationalism in the East.* New York: Harcourt, Brace, 1929.

MacCallum, Elizabeth P., *The Nationalist Crusade in Syria*. New York: Foreign Policy Association, 1928.

Mathews, Basil, *The Clash of World Forces: A Study in Nationalism, Bolshevism, and Christianity*. New York: Abingdon, 1931.

Owen, David Edward, *Imperialism and Nationalism in the Far East*. New York: Holt, 1929. Berkshire Studies in European History.

Internationalism

Bentwich, Norman, *The Mandates System*. London: Longmans, 1930.

Davies, David, *The Problem of the Twentieth Century*. London: Benn, 1930.

Ferrero, Guglielmo, *The Unity of the World*. Foreword by Charles A. Beard. New York: Boni, 1930.

Fosdick, Raymond B., *The Old Savage in the New Civilization*. New York: Doubleday, Doran, 1928.

Gibbons, Herbert A., *Nationalism and Internationalism*. New York: Stokes, 1930.

Hocking, William Ernest, "The Working of the Mandates" (in *The Yale Review*, Volume XIX, No. 2; New Haven, December, 1929).

Masaryk, T. G., *L'Idéal d'Humanité*. Paris: Rivière, 1930.

Paton, William, "The Federation and Internationalism" (in *The Student World*, Volume XXII, No. 3; Geneva, July, 1929).

Prescott, Donald A., *Education and International Relations*. Cambridge: Harvard University Press, 1930.

Randall, John Herman, *A World Community: The Supreme Task of the Twentieth Century*. New York: Stokes, 1930.

Stawell, F. Melian, *The Growth of International Thought*. London: Butterworth, 1929.

STRATTON, GEORGE MALCOLM, *Social Psychology of International Conduct.* New York: Appleton, 1929.

Ten Years of World Coöperation. Geneva: Secretariat of the League; Boston: World Peace Foundation, 1930.

TOYNBEE, ARNOLD J., and V. M. BOULTER, *Survey of International Relations 1929.* New York: Oxford University Press, 1930.

VAN KIRK, WALTER W., *Highways to International Good Will.* New York: Abingdon, 1930.

Economic

ARNOLD, JULEAN, *Some Bigger Issues in China's Problems.* Foreword by Hue Shih. Shanghai: Commercial Press, 1928.

CHEN, GIDEON, "Evangelism and Economic Life" (in *The Chinese Recorder,* Volume LXI, No. 1; Shanghai, January, 1930).

COLTON, ETHAN T., *The X Y Z of Communism.* New York: Macmillan, 1931.

DAS, RAJANI KANTA, "The Problem of India's Poverty" (in *The Modern Review,* Volume XLVII, No. 10; Calcutta, October, 1929).

DINGMAN, MARY A., "The Human Cost of Industry: Some Illustrations" (in *The Student World,* Volume XX, No. 4; Geneva, October, 1927).

EDDY, SHERWOOD, *The Challenge of Russia.* New York: Farrar & Rinehart, 1931.

HARADA, SHUICHI, *Labor Conditions in Japan.* New York: Columbia University Press, 1928.

KAGAWA, TOYOHIKO, "Marxism Advances on Japan" (in *The Christian Century,* Volume XLVI, No. 2; Chicago, January 10, 1929).

KENNEDY, M. D., *The Changing Fabric of Japan.* New York: Smith, 1931.

Koo, T. Z., "China in the Remaking" (in *The Annals of the American Academy of Political and Social Science*, Volume CLII; Philadelphia, November, 1930).

Macmillan, William M., *Complex South Africa*. London: Faber, 1930.

Oldham, J. H., *White and Black in Africa*. London: Longmans, 1930.

Smuts, J. C., *Africa and Some World Problems*. Oxford: Clarendon, 1930.

Thompson, Warren S., *Danger Spots in World Population*. New York: Knopf, 1929.

Visvesvaraya, M., "The Economic Condition of India" (in *The Indian Social Reformer*, Volume XLI, No. 17; Bombay, December 27, 1930).

Uplift of Women

Burton, Margaret E., *New Paths for Old Purposes*. New York: Missionary Education Movement, 1927.

——, *Women Workers of the Orient*. West Medford, Mass.: The Central Committee on the United Study of Foreign Missions, 1918.

Caton, A. R., Editor, *The Key of Progress: A Survey of the Status and Conditions of Women in India*, by Several Contributors. Foreword by H. E. the Lady Irwin. London: Oxford University Press, 1930.

Cousins, Margaret E., *The Awakening of Asian Womanhood*. Madras: Ganesh, 1922.

De Forest, Charlotte B., *The Woman and the Leaven in Japan*. West Medford, Mass.: The Central Committee on the United Study of Foreign Missions, 1923.

Faust, Allen K., *The New Japanese Womanhood*. New York: Doran, 1926.

GEDGE, EVELYN C., and MITHAN CHOKSI, Compilers and Editors, *Women in Modern India, Fifteen Papers by Indian Writers*. Bombay: D. B. Taraporewala Sons & Co., 1929.

HALIDÉ EDIB, *Memoirs of Halidé Edib*. New York: Century, 1926.

———, *The Turkish Ordeal; Being Further Memoirs of Halidé Edib*. New York: Century, 1928.

NEWELL, JANE I., "The Chinese Family: An Arena of Conflicting Cultures" (in *Social Forces, a Scientific Medium of Social Study and Interpretation*, Volume IX, No. 4; Chapel Hill, N. C., June, 1931).

PATRICK, MARY MILLS, *Under Five Sultans*. New York: Century, 1929.

PHILIPS, DAISY GRIGGS, "The Awakening of Egypt's Womanhood" (in *The Moslem World*, Volume XVIII, No. 4; New York, October, 1928).

PYE, EDITH M., "The Women's Movement in China" (in *The Asiatic Review*, n. s., Volume XXV, No. 82; London, April, 1929).

SMITH, MARGARET, "The Women's Movement in the Near and Middle East" (in *The Asiatic Review*, n. s., Volume XXIV, No. 78; London, April, 1928).

"Turkish Women as Pioneers, by a Western Woman Resident in Turkey" (in *The International Review of Missions*, Volume XVII, No. 68; London and New York, October, 1928).

UNDERHILL, MRS. L. A. [Mrs. Starr, of Peshawar], "Women and New Movements in India" (in *The Asiatic Review*, n. s., Volume XXVI, No. 85; London, January, 1930).

VAN DOREN, ALICE B., "Modern Movements Among Women in India" (in *The International Review of Missions*, Volume XVII, No. 66; London and New York, April, 1928).

Women in Industry in the Orient, A Source Book Compiled by

the Education and Research Division and the Industrial
Department of the Y. W. C. A. New York: Womans Press,
1925.

WOODSMALL, RUTH F., *The Changing Status of Moslem Women;
a Study made under a Rockefeller Foundation Fellowship.*

Education

BALME, HAROLD, "The Future of Christian Education in
China: From the Chinese Standpoint" (in *The International
Review of Missions*, Volume XIV, No. 55; London and New
York, July, 1925).

BROOKES, EDGAR H., *Native Education in South Africa.* Pretoria: van Schaik, 1930.

Christian Education in China. A Study Made by an Educational Commission Representing the Mission Boards and
Societies Conducting Work in China (E. D. Burton, Chairman). New York: Committee of Reference and Counsel of
the Foreign Missions Conference, 1922.

CRESSY, EARL HERBERT, . . . *Christian Higher Education in
China: A Study for the Year 1925-26.* . . . Shanghai, China:
China Christian Educational Association, 1928. (China
Christian Educational Association Bulletin No. 20, 1928.)
——, and C. C. CHIH, *Middle School Standards.* Shanghai:
East China Christian Education Association, 1929.

GENERAL COMMITTEE OF THE NEAR EAST SURVEY. *The Near
East and American Philanthropy.* New York: Columbia
University Press, 1929.

GUGGISBERG, SIR GORDON, *The Future of the Negro.* London:
Student Christian Movement, 1929.

INDIA, EDUCATION DEPARTMENT, *Progress of Education in India.
Quinquennial Review.* Calcutta, 1929.

INDIAN STATUTORY COMMISSION, *Interim Report (Review of the Growth of Education in British India by the Auxiliary Committee Appointed by the Commission)*, September, 1929. London: His Majesty's Stationery Office, 1929.

JONES, THOMAS JESSE, *Education in East Africa: A Study of East, Central, and South Africa by the Second African Education Commission under the Auspices of the Phelps-Stokes Fund, in Coöperation with the International Education Board*. New York: Phelps-Stokes Fund, 1925.

MCKEE, WILLIAM J., *New Schools for Young India: A Survey of Educational, Economic, and Social Conditions in India with Special Reference to More Effective Education*. Chapel Hill: University of North Carolina Press, 1930.

MAYHEW, ARTHUR INNES, *Christianity and the Government of India: An Examination of the Christian Forces at Work in the Administration of India and of the Mutual Relations of the British Government and Christian Missions, 1600–1920*. London: Faber & Gwyer, 1929.

MONROE, PAUL, *China: A Nation in Evolution*. New York: Macmillan, 1928.

——, *Essays in Comparative Education*. New York: Teachers College, Columbia University, 1927.

OLDHAM, J. H., "The Crisis in Christian Education in the Mission Field" (in *Papers on Educational Problems in Mission Fields*). London: International Missionary Council, 1921. (Pam.)

——, "Educational Policy of the British Government in Africa" (in *The International Review of Missions*, Volume XIV, No. 55; London and New York, July, 1925).

PHILIPPINE ISLANDS, BOARD OF EDUCATIONAL SURVEY, *A Survey of the Educational System of the Philippine Islands*. Manila: Bureau of Printing, 1925.

STUART, J. LEIGHTON, "Current Religious Issues as Faced at Yenching University" (in *Educational Review*, a Quarterly Journal Published by The China Christian Educational Association, Volume XXIII, No. 1, January, 1931).

——, *The Future of Missionary Education in China*. Reprinted from *The Chinese Students' Monthly*, Volume XXI, No. 6, April, 1926. (Pam.)

UNDERWOOD, HORACE HORTON, *Modern Education in Korea*. New York: International Press, 1926.

WILSON, FLORENCE, *Near East Educational Survey. Report of a Survey made during the months of April, May, and June, 1927*. London: Published for the European Center of the Carnegie Endowment for International Peace by the Hogarth Press, 1928.

Religion

ANESAKI, MASAHARA, *The Religious and Social Problems of the Orient*. New York: Macmillan, 1923.

ANDREWS, C. F., *Mahatma Gandhi's Ideas*. London: Allen & Unwin, 1929.

The Christian Approach to the Jew: . . . A Report of Conferences . . . held at Budapest and Warsaw in April, 1927. London: Edinburgh House, 1927.

Christians and Jews: A Report of the Atlantic City Conference on the Christian Approach to the Jews, May 12–15, 1931. New York: International Missionary Council, 1931.

COLTON, ETHAN T., *The X Y Z of Communism*. New York: Macmillan, 1931.

DEWICK, E. C., "Thought-Tendencies in Modern India" (in *The Guardian*, Volume IX, Nos. 17 and 18; Calcutta, April 30 and May 7, 1931).

EDDY, SHERWOOD, *The Challenge of Russia*. New York: Farrar & Rinehart, 1931.

GAIRDNER, W. H. T., "Christianity and Islam" (in *The Christian Life and Message in Relation to Non-Christian Systems of Thought and Life*. The Jerusalem Meeting of the International Missionary Council, March 24–April 8, 1928, Volume I). New York: International Missionary Council, 1928. Chapter VI.

JONES, RUFUS M., "Secular Civilization and the Christian Task" (in *The Christian Life and Message in Relation to Non-Christian Systems of Thought and Life*. The Jerusalem Meeting of the International Missionary Council, March 24–April 8, 1928, Volume I). New York: International Missionary Council, 1928. Chapter VII.

LAMMENS, HENRI, *Islam: Beliefs and Institutions;* translated from the French by Sir E. Denison Ross. London: Methuen, 1929.

LYON, D. WILLARD, "Religious Values in Confucianism" (in *The Christian Life and Message in Relation to Non-Christian Systems of Thought and Life*. The Jerusalem Meeting of the International Missionary Council, March 24–April 8, 1928, Volume I). New York: International Missionary Council, 1928. Chapter III.

MACKAY, JOHN A., "The Ecumenical Spirit and the Recognition of Christ" (in *The International Review of Missions*, Volume XVIII, No. 71; London and New York, July, 1929).

MACNICOL, NICOL, "Christianity and Hinduism" (in *The Christian Life and Message in Relation to Non-Christian Systems of Thought and Life*. The Jerusalem Meeting of the International Missionary Council, March 24–April 8, 1928, Volume I). New York: International Missionary Council, 1928. Chapter I.

MATHEWS, BASIL, *Young Islam on Trek*. New York: Friendship Press, 1926.

MORRISON, S. A., "New Developments in Moslem Lands" (in *The Moslem World*, Volume XVIII, No. 3; New York, July, 1928).

MOTT, JOHN R., Editor, *The Moslem World of To-Day*. New York: Doran, 1925.

NITOBÉ, INAZO, "The Penetration of the Life and Thought of Japan by Christianity" (in *The Japan Christian Quarterly*, Volume IV, No. 4; Tokyo, October, 1929).

PALLEN, CONDÉ B., and JOHN J. WYNNE, Editors, *The New Catholic Dictionary*. New York: Universal Knowledge Foundation, 1929.

PRATT, JAMES BISSETT, *The Pilgrimage of Buddhism and a Buddhist Pilgrimage*. London: Macmillan, 1928.

REISCHAUER, A. K., "Christianity and Northern Buddhism" (in *The Christian Life and Message in Relation to Non-Christian Systems of Thought and Life*. The Jerusalem Meeting of the International Missionary Council, March 24–April 8, 1928, Volume I). New York: 1928. Chapter V.

RICHTER, JULIUS, *Mission und Evangelisation im Orient*. Gütersloh: Bertelsmann, 1930.

SAUNDERS, KENNETH J., "Christianity and Buddhism" (in *The Christian Life and Message in Relation to Non-Christian Systems of Thought and Life*. The Jerusalem Meeting of the International Missionary Council, March 24–April 8, 1928, Volume I). New York: 1928. Chapter IV.

STUART, JOHN LEIGHTON, "Christianity and Confucianism" (in *The Christian Life and Message in Relation to Non-Christian Systems of Thought and Life*. The Jerusalem Meeting of the International Missionary Council, March 24–April 8, 1928, Volume I). New York: 1928. Chapter II.

STUART, JOHN LEIGHTON, "One of the Present Dangers to Protestant Christianity in China" (in *The Chinese Recorder*, Volume LXII, No. 5; Shanghai, May, 1931).

TITUS, MURRAY THURSTON, *Indian Islam; a Religious History of Islam in India*. London: Oxford University Press, 1930.

ZWEMER, SAMUEL M., *Across the World of Islam; Studies in Aspects of the Mohammedan Faith and in the Present Awakening of the Moslem Multitudes*. New York: Revell, 1929.

CHAPTER II

"Answers Tendered on Behalf of the National Christian Council of India, Burma, and Ceylon to the Questionnaire of the Royal Agricultural Commission" (in *The National Christian Council Review*, Volume XLVII, No. 2; Mysore City, February, 1927).

AZARIAH, V. S., Bishop of Dornakal, "The People of the Villages" (in *The Christian Task in India*, edited by John McKenzie). London: Macmillan, 1929. Chapter III.

——, and HENRY WHITEHEAD, Formerly Bishop of Madras, *Christ in the Indian Villages*. London: Student Christian Movement, 1930.

BRAYNE, FRANK LUGARD, *The Remaking of Village India*. London: Oxford University Press, 1929. 2d ed.

BRUNNER, EDMUND DE SCHWEINITZ, "Rural Korea: A Preliminary Survey of Economic, Social, and Religious Conditions" (in *The Christian Mission in Relation to Rural Problems*. The Jerusalem Meeting of the International Missionary Council, March 24–April 8, 1928, Volume VI). New York: International Missionary Council, 1928. Chapter IV.

BUCK, JOHN LOSSING, *Chinese Farm Economy. A Study of 2,866 Farms in Seventeen Localities and Seven Provinces in China*. Chicago: University of Chicago Press, 1930.

Buck, Mrs. Pearl S., *The Good Earth*. New York: Day, 1931.

Butterfield, Kenyon L., *The Christian Mission in Rural India*. New York: International Missionary Council, 1930.

——, *Report . . . on Rural Conditions and Sociological Problems in South Africa*. New York: Carnegie Corporation, 1929.

Christian Mission in Relation to Rural Problems, The. The Jerusalem Meeting of the International Missionary Council, March 24–April 8, 1928, Volume VI. New York: 1928.

Darling, M. L., *Rusticus Loquitur; or The Old Light and the New in the Punjab Village*. New York: Oxford University Press, 1930.

Findings for the Jerusalem Meeting, March 24–April 8, 1928. Tokyo: National Christian Council of Japan. (Pam.)

Higginbottom, Sam, *The Gospel and the Plow; or The Old Gospel and Modern Farming in Ancient India*. New York: Macmillan, 1921.

——, "The Problem of Poverty" (in *The Christian Task in India*, edited by John McKenzie). London: Macmillan, 1929. Chapter IX.

Hodge, J. Z., "Things That Hinder the Realization of the Ideal of a Rural Christian Community" (in *The National Christian Council Review*, Volume L, No. 8; Mysore City, August, 1930).

Hunnicut, Benjamin H., *Agricultural Missions*. New York: Friendship Press, 1931.

Japan Christian Quarterly. Special Rural Number, Volume VI, No. 2; Tokyo, April, 1931.

Kagawa, Toyohiko, "The Coöperative Movement in Japan and Its Part in the Christian Social Programme" (in *The Japan Christian Quarterly*, Volume V, No. 3; Tokyo, July, 1930).

McConnell, Charles M., *The Rural Billion*. New York: Friendship Press, 1931.

Near East Foundation: A Twentieth Century Concept of Practical Philanthropy. New York: Near East Foundation, n. d. (Pam.)

Paul, K. T., "The Development of a Rural Civilization" (in *The National Christian Council Review*, Volume L, No. 10; Mysore City, October, 1930).

Phillips, Ray E., *The Bantu Are Coming: Phases of South Africa's Race Problem*. London: Student Christian Movement, 1930.

Report of the Rural Conference held at Coimbatore, December 19 and 20, 1928. Poona: The National Christian Council of India, Burma, and Ceylon. (Pam.)

Royal Commission on Agriculture, India, *Abridged Report*. Bombay: Government Central Press, 1928.

Sugiyama, M., "A Study of the Rural Problem" (in *The Japan Mission Year Book*, edited by Paul S. Mayer). Tokyo: Kyo Bun Kwan, 1930. Chapter XVIII.

Van Doren, A., Editor, *Fourteen Experiments in Rural Education*. Calcutta: Association Press, 1928.

Village Education in India. The Report of a Commission of Inquiry (A. G. Fraser, Chairman). London: Oxford University Press, 1920.

Chapter III

Anderson, Adelaide May, *Humanity and Labour in China*. London: Student Christian Movement, 1928.

Anet, Henri, "Economic Development and Welfare of Natives: Theory and Practice in the Belgian Congo" (in *The International Review of Missions*, Volume XVII, No. 68; London and New York, October, 1928).

BURTON, MARGARET E., *New Paths for Old Purposes.* New York: Missionary Education Movement, 1927.

Christian Mission in Relation to Industrial Problems, The. The Jerusalem Meeting of the International Missionary Council, March 24–April 8, 1928, Volume V. New York: International Missionary Council, 1928.

DAS, RAJANI KANTA, *The Industrial Efficiency of India.* London: King, 1930.

FELDMAN, HERMAN, *Racial Factors in American Industry . . . based in part on a study made by the Inquiry, under the direction of Bruno Lasker,* with a foreword by Raymond B. Fosdick. New York: Harpers, 1931.

"Findings of the Industrial Conference, Nagpur, December 9 and 10, 1930" (in *The National Christian Council Review,* Volume LI, No. 2; Mysore City, February, 1931).

FRANCE, WALTER F., *Industrialism in Japan.* With a Preface by Cecil, Bishop of Southampton. London: S. P. G., 1928.

GRIMSHAW, HAROLD A., "Economic and Industrial Implications of Jerusalem" (in *The Student World,* Volume XXI, No. 4; Geneva, October, 1928).

HARADA, SHUICHI, *Labor Conditions in Japan.* New York: Columbia University Press, 1928.

HARRIS, JOHN H., *Slavery or "Sacred Trust"?* Preface by Gilbert Murray. London: Williams and Norgate, 1926.

HINDER, ELEANOR M., "China's New Factory Law as Affecting Women and Children" (in *The Chinese Recorder,* Volume LXII, No. 3; Shanghai, March, 1931).

HO, FRANKLIN L., and HSIEN DING FONG, *Extent and Effects of Industrialization in China.* Tientsin: Chihli Press, 1929. (Pam.)

INTERNATIONAL LABOUR CONFERENCE, TWELFTH SESSION, GENEVA, 1929, *Forced Labour: Report and Draft Questionnaire.* Item III on the Agenda. Geneva: International Labour Office, 1929.

JABAVU, D. D. T., *The Segregation Fallacy.* Lovedale: Lovedale Institution Press, 1928.

KAGAWA, TOYOHIKO, "The Penetration of Japanese Industry by Christianity" (in *The Japan Christian Quarterly*, Volume IV, No. 4; Tokyo, October, 1929).

KELMAN, JANET HARVEY, *Labour in India: A Study of the Conditions of Indian Women in Modern Industry.* London: Allen & Unwin, 1923.

KIRK, JOHN, *The Economic Aspects of Native Segregation in South Africa.* With a Foreword by Dr. C. T. Loram. London: King, 1929.

LUGARD, LORD, "Forced Labour Convention of 1930" (in *The International Review of Missions*, Volume XIX, No. 76; London and New York, October, 1930).

MATHESON, M. CECILE, *Indian Industry, Yesterday, To-Day, and To-Morrow.* London: Oxford University Press, 1930.

MOELIA, S. G., "Zending en Industrie" (in *Zendingstijdschrift De Opwekker, Orgaan van de Ned.-Ind. Zendingsbond*, Volume LXXIII, No. 12; Modjowarno, East Java, December, 1928).

ORCHARD, JOHN E., *Japan's Economic Position: The Progress of Industrialization.* New York: McGraw-Hill, 1930.

REDFIELD, WILLIAM C., *Dependent America: A Study of the Economic Bases of Our International Relations.* Boston: Houghton Mifflin, 1926.

RICHTER, JULIUS, "Die Industrialisierung Asiens und Africas und die Aufgabe der Mission" (in *Neue Allgemeine Missionszeitschrift*, Volume V, No. 9; Berlin, September, 1928).

ROOME, W. J. W., *Can Africa Be Won?* London: A. & C. Black, 1927.

SIMON, KATHLEEN, *Slavery.* With a Preface by her husband, the Rt. Hon. Sir John Simon. London: Hodder and Stoughton, 1929.

TAYLER, J. B., *Farm and Factory in China.* London: Student Christian Movement, 1928.

CHAPTER IV

ALEXANDER, WILL W., "The Negro in the New South" (in *The Annals of the American Academy of Political and Social Science,* Volume CXXXX, No. 229; Philadelphia, November, 1928).

ANDREWS, C. F., "Towards the Solution of the Race Problem" (in *The Friend,* Volume LXX, No. 40; London, October 3, 1930).

BROWN, ARTHUR J., *Japan in the World of To-Day.* New York: Revell, 1928.

BRYCE, JAMES, *The Relations of the Advanced and Backward Races of Mankind.* The Romanes Lecture for 1902. London: Oxford University Press, 1903. 2d ed.

Christian Mission in the Light of Race Conflict, The. The Jerusalem Meeting of the International Missionary Council, March 24–April 8, 1928, Volume IV. New York: International Missionary Council, 1928.

Christian Students and Modern South Africa: A Report of the Bantu-European Student Christian Conference, Fort Hare, June 27–July 3, 1930. Fort Hare: Student Christian Association, 1930.

CONDLIFFE, J. B., *The Third Mediterranean in History. An Introduction to Pacific Problems.* Christchurch: Student Christian Movement of New Zealand, 1926. (Pam.)

ELEAZER, ROBERT B., *An Adventure in Faith: A Brief Story of the Interracial Movement in the South.* Atlanta: Commission on Interracial Coöperation, 1929. (Pam.)

GANDHI, M. K., *The Story of My Experiments with Truth.* Translated from the original in Gujarati by Mahadev Desai. Ahmedabad: Navajivan Press, 1927–29. 2 vol.

GULICK, SIDNEY L., *American Democracy and Asiatic Citizenship.* New York: Scribner's, 1918.

——, *Reëstablishment of Right Relations with Japan.* New York: Federal Council of Churches, 1925. (Pam.)

HOYLAND, JOHN S., *The Race Problem and the Teaching of Jesus Christ.* London: Religious Tract Society, 1925.

THE INQUIRY, *And Who Is My Neighbor? An Outline for the Study of Race Relations in America.* Part I. New York: Association Press, 1924.

JONES, THOMAS JESSE, *Education in East Africa: A Study of East, Central, and South Africa by the Second African Education Commission under the Auspices of the Phelps-Stokes Fund, in Coöperation with the International Education Board.* New York: Phelps-Stokes Fund, 1925.

KAWAKAMI, K. K., *The Real Japanese Question.* New York: Macmillan, 1921.

LASKER, BRUNO, *Filipino Immigration to Continental United States and to Hawaii.* Chicago: University of Chicago Press, for Institute of Pacific Relations, 1931.

LEYS, NORMAN, *Kenya,* ... with an Introduction by Gilbert Murray. London: Woolf, 1924.

LUGARD, LORD, *An Address . . . Upon Ten Years' Working of the Mandatory System, at the Annual Meeting of the Anti-Slavery and Aborigines Protection Society, May 29, 1930.* London: Anti-Slavery and Aborigines Protection Society. (Pam.)

MATHEWS, BASIL, *The Clash of Color: A Study in the Problem of Race.* New York: Missionary Education Movement, 1924.

MOTON, ROBERT RUSSA, *What the Negro Thinks.* Garden City: Doubleday, Doran, 1929.

MURPHY, EDGAR GARDNER, *The Basis of Ascendancy: A Discussion of Certain Principles of Public Policy Involved in the Development of the Southern States.* New York: Longmans, 1909.

OLDHAM, J. H., *Christianity and the Race Problem.* London: Student Christian Movement, 1924.

SMITH, EDWIN W., *Aggrey of Africa: A Study in Black and White.* London: Student Christian Movement, 1929.

SPEER, ROBERT E., *Race and Race Relations: A Christian View of Human Contacts.* New York: Revell, 1924.

STODDARD, LOTHROP, *The Rising Tide of Color against White World Supremacy,* with an Introduction by Madison Grant. New York: Scribner's, 1920.

Student World, The, Volume XIX, No. 3; Geneva, July, 1926. The entire number is devoted to different aspects of race relationships.

TOWNSEND, MEREDITH, *Asia and Europe: Studies Presenting the Conclusions Formed by the Author in a Long Life Devoted to the Subject.* New York: Putnam's, 1911. 4th ed.

WASHINGTON, BOOKER T., *Up from Slavery: An Autobiography.* New York: Young People's Missionary Movement, 1900.

WEATHERFORD, WILLIS DUKE, *The Negro from Africa to America.* New York: Doran, 1924.

CHAPTER V

ANDREWS, C. F., *Mahatma Gandhi's Ideas.* London: Allen & Unwin, 1929.

CHAO, T. C., "Needs That Western Christians Can Help Meet" (in *The Chinese Recorder*, Volume LX, No. 6; Shanghai, June, 1929).

CHEN, W. Y., "Types of Service Required in China" (in *Students and the Future of Christian Missions: Student Volunteer Convention, 1927–28*). New York: Student Volunteer Movement, 1928.

FLEMING, DANIEL JOHNSON, *Ways of Sharing with Other Faiths*. New York: Association Press, 1929.

GAIRDNER, W. H. T., "Oriental Christian Communities and the Evangelization of the Moslems" (in *The Moslem World of To-Day*, edited by John R. Mott). New York: Doran, 1925. Chapter XVIII.

HODGKIN, H. T., "The Missionary Situation in China" (in *Foreign Missions Conference of North America, Annual Report, 1928*). New York: 1928.

HOYLAND, JOHN S., "The Contribution of India to Western Religion" (in *The Friend*, Volume LXX, No. 40; London, October 3, 1930).

INMAN, SAMUEL G., "Young Churches in Old Lands" (in *The International Review of Missions*, Volume XIX, No. 73; London and New York, January, 1930).

JONES, E. STANLEY, "The Ashram Ideal" (in *Indian Church Problems of To-Day*, edited by Brenton Thoburn Badley). Madras: Methodist Publishing House, 1930. Chapter III.

LATOURETTE, KENNETH S., "Commission on Mission Policies and Methods in China" (in *Foreign Missions Conference of North America, Annual Report, 1929*). New York: 1929.

——, "What Is Happening to Missions?" (in *The Yale Review*, Volume XVIII, No. 1; New Haven, September, 1928).

LOBENSTINE, E. C., "Why Coöperative Ability?" (in *Far Horizons*, Volume XI, No. 4; New York, January, 1931).

McAFEE, CLELAND BOYD, *Changing Foreign Missions*. New York: Revell, 1927.

McFADYEN, J. F., *The Missionary Idea in Life and Religion*. New York: Scribner's, 1926.

MACNICOL, NICOL, *India in the Dark Wood*. London: Livingstone, 1930.

MONK, F. F., "The Interactions in Religious Thought of East and West" (in *The International Review of Missions*, Volume XVIII, No. 72; London and New York, October, 1929).

MORGAN, E. R., Editor, *Essays Catholic and Missionary*. London: S. P. C. K., 1928.

PHILIP, P. O., *Memorandum on "Devolution."* Poona: Scottish Mission, n. d. (Pam.)

RAWLINGS, E. H., "Report of Commission X on Relations between Foreign and National Workers" (in *Christian Work in South America: Official Report of the Congress on Christian Work in South America, Montevideo, Uruguay, April, 1925*). New York: Revell, 1925.

RAWLINSON, FRANK, *Western Money and the Chinese Church*. Shanghai: Presbyterian Mission Press, 1929.

Relation between the Younger and the Older Churches. The Jerusalem Meeting of the International Missionary Council, March 24–April 8, 1928, Volume III. New York: 1928.

"Relation between the Younger and Older Churches" (in *Findings for the Jerusalem Meeting, March 24–April 8, 1928*). Tokyo: National Christian Council of Japan. Chapter II. (Pam.)

RICHTER, JULIUS, "Die Tagung des Internationalen Missionsrates auf dem Ölberg bei Jerusalem vom 24. März bis 8. April 1928" (in *Neue Allgemeine Missionszeitschrift*, Volume V, Nos. 6, 7; Berlin, June, July, 1928).

SCHUURMAN, B. M., "De Verhouding van de Jongere tot de Oudere Kerken" (in *Zendingstijdschrift De Opwekker, Orgaan van den Ned.-Ind. Zendingsbond*, Volume LXXIII, No. 12; Modjowarno, East Java, December, 1928).

SELBIE, W. B., "*The Sadhu*" (in "Reviews of Books," *The International Review of Missions*, Volume XVI, No. 61; London and New York, January, 1927).

TSU, Y. Y., "International Sharing and Fellowship" (in *The Chinese Recorder*, Volume LX, No. 6; Shanghai, June, 1929).

"Younger and Older Churches" (in *Report of the Enlarged Meeting of the National Christian Council of India, Madras, December 28, 1928–January 2, 1929*). Poona: National Christian Council. Part VII.

CHAPTER VI

CHENG, C. Y., "The Chinese Church" (in *China To-Day Through Chinese Eyes*). London: Student Christian Movement, 1922. Chapter VII.

——, "The Development of an Indigenous Church in China" (in *The International Review of Missions*, Volume XII, No. 47; London and New York, July, 1923).

China Christian Year Book, 1929. Shanghai: Christian Literature Society, 1929.

Chinese Recorder, The, Volume LXII, No. 5, Shanghai, May, 1931, devoted to the topic: "The China Christian Espouses Social Evangelism."

Christian Worker in North China, The: Prepared by a Committee and Presented at the Peiping Regional Conference held under the auspices of the National Christian Council of China, Wo Fo Ssu, April 28–May 2, 1926. Shanghai.

Continuation Committee Conferences in Asia, 1912–1913. A Brief Account of the Conferences, together with their Findings and Lists of Members. New York: Published by the Chairman of the Continuation Committee, 1913.

Findings of the Bangkok Conference called by John R. Mott, Chairman of the International Missionary Council. Bangkok, Siam, February 27–March 4, 1929. Bangkok: 1929. (Pam.)

FLEMING, DANIEL JOHNSON, "Giving Way to Nationals" (in his *Whither Bound in Missions*). New York: Association Press, 1925. Chapter IX.

GERDINE, J. L., "Methodist Union—More Union?" (in *The Korea Mission Field*, Volume XXVII, No. 4; Seoul, April, 1931).

HAWKINS, F. H., *Report on Visit to China as a Special Deputation from the Directors, China Mission, London Missionary Society, August, 1927, to March, 1928.* London: Published by the Society, 1928.

Japan Mission Year Book, formerly *The Christian Movement in Japan and Formosa.* Tokyo: Kyo Bun Kwan, 1930.

LAUBACH, FRANK CHARLES, *The People of the Philippines: Their Religious Progress and Preparation for Spiritual Leadership in the Far East.* New York: Doran, 1925.

"The Methodist Church of Korea" (in *The Missionary Voice*, Volume XXI, No. 2; Milwaukee, February, 1931).

PATON, WILLIAM, "The Indigenous Church" (in *The International Review of Missions*, Volume XVI, No. 61; London and New York, January, 1927).

PHILIP, P. OOMMAN, "Experiments in Indian Expression of Christian Service" (in *The International Review of Missions*, Volume XVIII, No. 70; London and New York, April, 1929).

PHILIP, P. OOMMAN, "Indigenous Christian Efforts" (in *The Christian Task in India*, edited by John McKenzie). London: Macmillan, 1929. Chapter XII.

——, *Report on a Survey of Indigenous Christian Efforts in India, Burma, and Ceylon.* Poona, 1928. (Pam.)

PROTESTANT EPISCOPAL CHURCH IN THE U. S. A., BOARD OF MISSIONS, *Report of the Commission to China, October, 1927–March, 1928.* New York: 1928. (Pam.)

RAWLINSON, FRANK, *Western Money and the Chinese Church.* Shanghai: Presbyterian Mission Press, 1929.

Relation between the Younger and the Older Churches. The Jerusalem Meeting of the International Missionary Council, March 24–April 8, 1928, Volume III. New York: 1928.

Report of Conference on the Church in China To-Day: The Report of a Conference of Christian Workers with Dr. John R. Mott, Chairman of the International Missionary Council, January 5–7, 1926. Shanghai: National Christian Council.

"Report of Corresponding Secretaries" (in *Annual Report of the Board of Foreign Missions of the Methodist Episcopal Church for the Year 1930*). New York: 1931.

"Some Official Statements on Devolution" (in *The Relation between the Younger and the Older Churches.* The Jerusalem Meeting of the International Missionary Council, March 24–April 8, 1928, Volume III). New York: 1928. Appendix A.

SPEER, ROBERT E., "New Demands on the Mission Field Created by New World Conditions" (in his *The Church and Missions*). New York: Doran, 1926. Chapter V.

——, and RUSSELL CARTER, *Report on India and Persia of the Deputation sent by the Board of Foreign Missions of the Presbyterian Church in the U. S. A. to Visit These Fields in 1921–22.* New York: 1922.

——, and HUGH T. KERR, *Report on Japan and China of the Deputation Sent by the Board of Foreign Missions of the Presbyterian Church in the U. S. A. to Visit These Fields and Attend a Series of Evaluation Conferences in China in 1926.* New York: 1927.

WADDY, STACY, "The Younger and Older Churches" (in *The International Review of Missions*, Volume XVII, No, 68; London and New York, October, 1928).

WARNSHUIS, A. L., "Church Union" (in *Christian World Facts*, November, 1930, No. 13; New York: Foreign Missions Conference of North America).

WORLD MISSIONARY CONFERENCE, EDINBURGH, 1910, *Report of Commission II: The Church in the Mission Field.* New York: Revell, 1910. Volume II.

CHAPTER VII

AINSLIE, PETER, *The Scandal of Christianity.* New York: Willet, Clark & Colby, 1929.

BATE, H. N., Editor, *Faith and Order: Proceedings of the World Conference, Lausanne, August 3–21, 1927.* London: Student Christian Movement, 1927.

VAN BOETZELAER VAN DUBBELDAM, BARON C. W. TH., "Was kann die kontinentale Gruppe tun, um ihren Beitrag zur internationalen Arbeitsgemeinschaft zu leisten?" (in *Verhandlungen der XV. Kontinentalen Missionskonferenz zu Bremen vom 14. bis 18. Mai 1925*). Bremen: Kommissionsverlag der Norddeutschen Missions-Gesellschaft, 1925.

Call for Christian Unity: The Challenge of a World Situation. London: Hodder and Stoughton, 1930. Especially "The Movement toward Unity in China," by Francis Cho-Min Wei, "In Persia," by J. H. Linton, and "In India," by A. W. Davies.

Christian Education in China. A Study Made by an Educational Commission Representing the Mission Boards and Societies Conducting Work in China (E. D. Burton, Chairman). New York: Committee of Reference and Counsel of the Foreign Missions Conference, 1922.

Church of Christ in China: Achievements and Immediate Tasks: The Address of the General Secretary to the Second Assembly, Canton, China, October 26–November 8, 1930. Signed A. R. Kepler, General Secretary. Canton, October 27, 1930. (Pam.)

Church Union, News and Views. Organ of the Continuation Committee of the South India Joint Committee on Union. Madras: The Christian Literature Society for India, Volume I, July, 1930, to date.

Conference of Missionary Societies in Great Britain and Ireland. Report of Sixteenth Annual Conference, The Hayes, Swanwick, June 14–18, 1927. London: Edinburgh House, 1927.

CRESSY, EARL H., *Christian Higher Education in China.* Shanghai: China Christian Educational Association, 1928.

GARVIE, ALFRED E., *The Reunion of the Christian Churches: Hopes and Hindrances.* Reprinted from *The Contemporary Review,* April, 1930. (Pam.)

GOLLOCK, G. A., "Fifteen Years' Growth: A Study in Missionary Coöperation" (in *The International Review of Missions,* Volume XV, No. 57; London and New York, January, 1926).

International Missionary Coöperation. The Jerusalem Meeting of the International Missionary Council, March 24–April 8, 1928, Volume VII. New York: International Missionary Council, 1928.

Jones, Mark M., *A Missionary Audit*. Reprinted from *The Atlantic Monthly*, December, 1927. (Pam.)

Linton, J. H., "Towards a United National Church of Persia" (in *The Church Overseas*, Volume III, No. 10; London, April, 1930).

Maclennan, Kenneth, *Twenty Years of Missionary Coöperation*. London: Edinburgh House, 1927.

Marchant, Sir James, Editor, *The Reunion of Christendom: A Survey of the Present Position*. New York: Henry Holt and Company, 1929. Especially "Church Union in Scotland," by Alexander Martin, "The United Church of Canada," by T. Albert Moore, and "The Anglican Church in India," by the Bishop of Dornakal.

Mathews, Basil, and Harry Bisseker, *Fellowship in Thought and Prayer*. London: Student Christian Movement, 1926. 2d rev. ed.

Methodist Church of Mexico: The Report of the Joint Commission on Unification in Mexico. Mexico City, D. F., Mexico, July 7, 8, 1930, issued by the Authority of the Commission.

Moss, Leslie B., *Adventures in Missionary Coöperation*. New York: Foreign Missions Conference, 1930.

Mott, John R., "A Creative International Fellowship" (in *The International Review of Missions*, Volume XVII, No. 67; London and New York, July, 1928.)

——, "International Missionary Coöperation; Conditions Underlying Successful International Coöperation" (in *The International Review of Missions*, Volume XI, No. 41; London and New York, January, 1922).

Palmer, Edwin James, "Union of Churches in South India: The Present Position" (in *The Church Overseas*, Volume III, No. 10; London, April, 1930).

PATTON, CORNELIUS H., "A World Program of Christian Literature" (in *The International Review of Missions*, Volume XI, No. 44; London and New York, October, 1922).

"Proclamation Regarding the Unification and Organization of the Korean Methodist Church" (in *The Korean Mission Field*, Volume XXVII, No. 1; Seoul, January, 1931).

Review of the Churches: A Constructive Quarterly. Volume VII, No. 1; London, January, 1930. "Church Union in Southern India."

RITSON, JOHN H., *Christian Literature in the Mission Field: A Survey of the Present Situation Made under the Direction of the Continuation Committee of the World Missionary Conference, 1910.* Edinburgh: Continuation Committee, 1910.

ROOTS, LOGAN H., "The Problem of Reunion in China" (in *The Church Overseas*, Volume II, No. 7; London, July, 1929).

RYANG, J. S., "The Future of the Korean Methodist Church" (in *The Missionary Voice*, Volume XXI, No. 3; Milwaukee, March, 1931).

SLOSSER, GAIUS JACKSON, *Christian Unity: Its History and Challenge in All Communions, in All Lands.* New York: Dutton, 1929.

"Unity of the Church, The" (in *The Lambeth Conference, 1930*). London: S. P. C. K., 1930. Report of Committee III.

WALLER, E. H. M., *Church Union in South India.* London: S. P. C. K., 1929.

WILLIAMS, N. P., *Lausanne, Lambeth, and South India.* London: Longmans, 1930.

WOODS, EDWARD S., *Lausanne 1927: An Interpretation of the World Conference on Faith and Order Held at Lausanne August 3–21, 1927.* London: Student Christian Movement, 1927.

ZWEMER, SAMUEL M., "A United Christendom and Islam" (in *The Review of the Churches*, Volume V, No. 2; London, April, 1928).

CHAPTER VIII

BATES, C. L. J., "The One Million Souls Campaign" (in *The Japan Christian Quarterly*, Volume IV, No. 1; Tokyo, January, 1929).

BROWN, WILLIAM ADAMS, *Humanism: What It Is and How to Meet It*. An Address delivered at the Foreign Missions Conference, Atlantic City, New Jersey, January 15, 1930. New York: Foreign Missions Conference. (Pam.)

BUCK, OSCAR M., "How Can Christians Adequately Confront the World's Life with Its Need of Christ?" (in *Foreign Missions Conference of North America, Annual Report, 1930*). New York: 1930.

CAIRNS, DAVID S., "The Christian Message: A Comparison of Thought in 1910 and 1928" (in *The International Review of Missions*, Volume XVIII, No. 71; London and New York, July, 1929).

——, *The Reasonableness of the Christian Faith*. London: Hodder and Stoughton, 1918.

Christian Life and Message in Relation to Non-Christian Systems of Thought and Life. The Jerusalem Meeting of the International Missionary Council, March 24–April 8, 1928, Volume I. New York: International Missionary Council, 1928.

DAVIS, OZORA S., "Life-Giving Convictions" (in *The Christian Advocate*, Volume CIV, No. 25; New York, June 20, 1929).

EBIZAWA, AKIRA, "The Kingdom of God Movement—Its Story to Date" (in *The Japan Christian Quarterly*, Volume V, No. 3; Tokyo, July, 1930).

FARQUHAR, J. N., *The Crown of Hinduism.* London: Milford, 1913.

FLEMING, DANIEL JOHNSON, *Attitudes toward Other Faiths.* New York: Association Press, 1928.

FRICK, HEINRICH, "Is a Conviction of the Superiority of His Message Essential to the Missionary?" (in *The International Review of Missions,* Volume XV, No. 60; London and New York, October, 1926).

HALL, CHARLES CUTHBERT, *Christ and the Eastern Soul. The Witness of the Oriental Consciousness to Jesus Christ.* The Barrows Lectures, 1906-07. Chicago: University of Chicago Press, 1909.

HARTENSTEIN, KARL, "The Theology of the Word and Missions" (in *The International Review of Missions,* Volume XX, No. 78; London and New York, April, 1931).

HEIM, KARL, "The Message of the New Testament to the Non-Christian World" (in *The International Review of Missions,* Volume XVII, No. 65; London and New York, January, 1928).

JONES, E. STANLEY, *Christ at the Round Table.* London: Hodder and Stoughton, 1928.

——, *The Christ of the Indian Road.* New York: Abingdon, 1925.

——, "Open Letter to Mr. Gandhi" (in *The National Christian Council Review,* Volume LI, No. 5; Mysore City, May, 1931. Reprinted from *The Fellowship,* April, 1931).

JONES, RUFUS M., "Secular Civilization and the Christian Task" (in *The Christian Life and Message in Relation to Non-Christian Systems of Thought and Life.* The Jerusalem Meeting of the International Missionary Council, March 24–April 8, 1928, Volume I). New York: International Missionary Council, 1928. Chapter VII.

KRAEMER, H., "Christianity and Secularism" (in *The International Review of Missions*, Volume XIX, No. 74; London and New York, April, 1930).

LARSEN, L. P., "The Meaning of Conversion—A Christian View" (in *Conversion and Coöperation in Religion*). Madras: Madras International Fellowship, 1929. Chapter II. (Pam.)

LATOURETTE, KENNETH S., "The Real Issue in Foreign Missions" (in *The Christian Century*, Volume XLVIII, No. 15; Chicago, April 15, 1931).

MACKAY, JOHN A., "Reflections on the Christian Message in the Present World Drama" (in *The Student World*, Volume XXIII, No. 3; Geneva, July, 1930).

PATON, WILLIAM, *A Faith for the World*. Edinburgh: Turnbull and Spears, 1929.

PIETERS, ALBERTUS, *A Plea for World-Wide Newspaper and Correspondence Evangelism*. New Haven: 1920. (Pam.)

RAWLINSON, FRANK, "Training and Developing Good Writers" (in *Foreign Missions Conference of North America, Annual Report, 1925*). New York: 1925.

Religious Education. The Jerusalem Meeting of the International Missionary Council, March 24–April 8, 1928, Volume II. New York: International Missionary Council, 1928.

SAUNDERS, KENNETH, *The Gospel for Asia*. New York: Macmillan, 1928.

SMITH, EDWIN W., *The Shrine of a People's Soul*. London: Church Missionary Society, 1929.

SOCKMAN, RALPH W., *Morals of To-Morrow*. New York: Harpers, 1931.

SOPER, EDMUND D., "The Unique and Distinctive Elements in Christianity" (in *Foreign Missions Conference of North America, Annual Report, 1928*). New York: 1928.

SPEER, ROBERT E., *Some Living Issues.* New York: Revell, 1930.

TEMPLE, WILLIAM, ARCHBISHOP OF YORK, "Missions and Theology" (in *The Church Overseas,* Volume III, No. 10; London, April, 1930).

Theology and the Christian World Mission: A Short Report of a Conference on the Preparation of the Ministry, held at York, April 2 to 5, 1929. Signed by William Ebor, J. H. Oldham, and William Paton. London: Conference of Missionary Societies in Great Britain and Ireland; International Missionary Council, 1929. (Pam.)

WALTON, W. H. MURRAY, "The Secular Press as an Evangelistic Agency" (in *The International Review of Missions,* Volume XVIII, No. 69; London and New York, January, 1929).

CHAPTER IX

ABRAHAM, J. S. B., "Are Christian Missions Still Needed in India?" (in *The Student World,* Volume XXI, No. 2; Geneva, March, 1928).

ANTHONY, A. W., Editor, *Changing Conditions in Public Giving: Papers and Conclusions. Third Conference on Financial and Fiduciary Matters, Hotel Chalfonte, Atlantic City, N. J., March 19-21, 1929.* New York: Federal Council of Churches, 1929.

ARCHER, JOHN CLARK, *A New Approach in Missionary Education.* New York: Missionary Education Movement, 1926.

Brennende Fragen der Frauenmission. Leipzig: Mädchen-Bibel-Kreise, 1928. (Pam.)

BROWN, INA C., *Training for World Friendship.* Nashville: Cokesbury, 1929.

Building the Christian World Society. A Suggested Policy in Missionary Education Growing Out of a Memorandum Presented by Francis P. Miller to the National Council of Student Associations at Chestnut Hill, Pa., September, 1924. New York: Association Press, 1924. (Pam.)

Call for Colleagues from Leaders in the Younger Christian Churches. New York: Student Volunteer Movement, 1930. (Pam.)

CAPEN, SAMUEL B., *The American Laymen's Missionary Movement: An Address.* London: Oliphant, 1907. (Pam.)

CAVERT, SAMUEL McCREA, *The Adventure of the Church.* New York: Missionary Education Movement, 1927.

"Character Qualities Needed by a Foreign Missionary" (in *Far Horizons*, Volume XI, No. 1; New York, October, 1930).

DIFFENDORFER, R. E., "The World Mission of Christianity and the Modern Preacher" (in *The International Review of Missions*, Volume XIX, No. 75; New York, July, 1930).

DODD, E. M., *Physical Fitness and Foreign Service.* New York: Student Volunteer Movement, n. d. (Pam.)

FAHS, CHARLES H., *Trends in Protestant Giving. A Study of Church Finance in the United States.* New York: Institute of Social and Religious Research, 1929. (Pam.)

FLEMING, DANIEL JOHNSON, "Eradicating a Sense of Superiority" (in his *Whither Bound in Missions*). New York: Association Press, 1925. Chapter I.

FREITAG, ANTON, *Akademiker und Mission.* Münster: Aschendorff, 1927. (Pam.)

GATES, HERBERT WRIGHT, *Missionary Education in the Church.* Boston: Pilgrim Press, 1928.

HALFORD, E. W., "The Place of the Laity in the Church." Report of Commission II (in *Lake Geneva Conference, 1911*). New York: Laymen's Missionary Movement, 1911.

HARRISON, PAUL W., *Preparation for Missionary Service*. New York: Student Volunteer Movement, n. d. (Pam.)

HODGKIN, HENRY T., *Students and the Foreign Service of the Kingdom of God*. London: Student Volunteer Missionary Union, n. d. (Pam.)

JACKA, H. T., *A Mind for the Kingdom*. London: Edinburgh House, 1928.

KELLY, JOHN BAILEY, "Missionary Education for Men" (in *The International Journal of Religious Education*, Volume VI, No. 5; Chicago, February, 1930).

LATOURETTE, KENNETH SCOTT, *What Can I Believe about Foreign Missions?* New York: Student Volunteer Movement, n. d. (Pam.)

Leaders' Handbook Series. New York: Missionary Education Movement.

MCAFEE, CLELAND BOYD, *Christian Message and Program*. Philadelphia: Presbyterian Board of Christian Education, 1929.

MATHEWS, BASIL, "Youth and the Human Scene" (in *Far Horizons*, Volume XI, No. 7; New York, April, 1931).

MILLAR, WILLIAM B., "The Advance of a Decade—Decennial Report of the General Secretary" (in *Men and World Service; Addresses delivered at the National Missionary Congress, Washington, D. C., April 26-30, 1916*). New York: Laymen's Missionary Movement, 1916.

PALMER, LEON C., *The Ministry of Laymen—A Plea for Lay Evangelism*. Philadelphia: Brotherhood of St. Andrew, 1927.

PERKINS, HENRY A., *The Case for Foreign Missions*. New York: Student Volunteer Movement, 1931. A Reprint from *The American Mercury*. (Pam.)

POTEAT, GORDON, Editor, *Students and the Future of Christian Missions*. Report of the Tenth Quadrennial Convention of the Student Volunteer Movement for Foreign Missions, Detroit, December 28, 1927, to January 1, 1928. New York: Student Volunteer Movement, 1928.

Purpose of God in the Life of the World: Being Some of the Addresses Delivered at a Conference on International and Missionary Questions, Liverpool, January 2-7, 1929; edited by Edward Shillito. London: Student Christian Movement, 1929. (Liverpool Quadrennial Conference of the Student Volunteer Missionary Union.)

RAM, B. L. RALLIA, "Are Christian Missions Still Needed in India?" (in *The Student World*, Volume XXI, No. 2; Geneva, March, 1928).

Reports of the Interdenominational Congress on Men's Work, Cincinnati, Ohio, December 11, 12, 1930. New York: Methodist Book Concern. (Pam.)

RYDER, A. R., *The Priesthood of the Laity*. Donnellan Lectures, 1907-08. London: Hodder and Stoughton, 1911.

SAILER, T. H. P., *The Mission Study Class Leader*. New York: Missionary Education Movement, 1921.

——, "The Task of Missionary Education as I See It" (in *The International Journal of Religious Education*, Volume VII, No. 2; Chicago, November, 1930).

——, "What Is Missionary Education?" (in *The International Review of Missions*, Volume XX, No. 78; London and New York, April, 1931).

SILVERTHORN, E. H., "The Woman's Part in the Missionary Program" (in *The International Journal of Religious Education*, Volume VI, No. 5; Chicago, February, 1930).

SÖRENSEN, ANNA, *Om Missionsundervisning*. Stockholm: Svenska Kyrkans Diakonistyrelsen Bokförlag, 1930.

SPEER, ROBERT E., "New Demands on the Foreign Mission Enterprise at the Home Base" (in his *The Church and Missions*). New York: Doran, 1926. Chapter IV.

Syllabus on Christian Missions, A. Built upon questions raised by students in conferences under the leadership of Dr. John R. Mott, October, 1929, to January, 1930, in twenty student centers throughout the United States and Canada. New York: Student Volunteer Movement. (Pam.)

TRIMBLE, H. B., *The Christian Motive and Method in Stewardship.* Nashville: Cokesbury, 1930.

WATSON, CHARLES R., "Ace High Missionaries" (in *Far Horizons*, Volume XI, No. 8; New York, May, 1931).

"Why Have Missionary Contributions Declined? A Symposium" (in *The Missionary Review of the World*, Volume LIII, No. 4; New York, April, 1930).

WILSON, JESSE R., *How Many New Missionaries Are Needed?* New York: Student Volunteer Movement, n. d. (Pam.)

——, *Jerusalem's Answer to Present-Day Inquiries.* New York: Student Volunteer Movement, n. d. (Pam.)

CHAPTER X

ARMSTRONG, SAMUEL CHAPMAN, *Education for Life*, with an Introduction by Francis Greenwood Peabody and a Biographical Note by Helen W. Ludlow. Hampton, Va.: Hampton Normal and Agricultural Institute, 1914.

BARBOUR, GEORGE F., *The Life of Alexander Whyte, D.D.* London: Hodder and Stoughton, 1923.

BLAIKIE, WILLIAM GARDEN, *The Personal Life of David Livingstone. Chiefly from His Unpublished Journals and Correspondence in the Possession of His Family.* New York: Harpers, 1881.

Book of Acts, The.

BRENT, CHARLES H., *Leadership*. William Belden Noble Lectures, 1907, Harvard University. New York: Longmans, 1908.

BRUCE, ALEXANDER BALMAIN, *The Training of the Twelve; or Passages Out of the Gospels Exhibiting the Twelve Disciples of Jesus under Discipline for the Apostleship*. Edinburgh: 1883. 3d ed.

BRYCE, JAMES BRYCE, VISCOUNT, *Studies in Contemporary Biography*. London: Macmillan, 1903.

CUSHING, HARVEY, *The Life of Sir William Osler*. Oxford: Clarendon, 1925. 2 vol.

DAVIS, JEROME D., *A Maker of New Japan* [Life of Joseph Hardy Neesima]. New York: Revell, 1905. 3d ed.

FOSTER, JOHN, *Decision of Character*. Introductory Note by John R. Mott. Abridged. New York: Student Volunteer Movement, n. d.

HARDY, ARTHUR SHERBURNE, *Life and Letters of Joseph Hardy Neesima*. Boston: Houghton Mifflin, 1894.

JUDSON, EDWARD, *The Life of Adoniram Judson*. New York: Randolph, 1883.

McGIFFERT, ARTHUR CUSHMAN, *Martin Luther: The Man and His Work*. New York: Century, 1911.

MATHEWS, BASIL, *Dr. Ralph Wardlaw Thompson*. London: Religious Tract Society, 1917.

MOODY, WILLIAM R., *D. L. Moody*. New York: Macmillan, 1930.

MORLEY, JOHN MORLEY, FIRST VISCOUNT, *The Life of William Ewart Gladstone*. New York: Macmillan, 1903. 3 vol.

Plutarch's Lives; The Translation called Dryden's, Corrected from the Greek and Revised by A. H. Clough. Boston: Little, Brown, 1910. 5 vol.

ROTHSCHILD, ALONZO, *Lincoln, Master of Men: A Study in Character*. Boston: Houghton Mifflin, 1906.

SEDGWICK, HENRY DWIGHT, *Ignatius Loyola: An Attempt at an Impartial Biography*. New York: Macmillan, 1923.

SMITH, EDWIN W., *Aggrey of Africa: A Study in Black and White*. London: Student Christian Movement, 1929.

STALKER, JAMES, *Imago Christi: The Example of Jesus Christ*. Introduction by Rev. W. M. Taylor. New York: Armstrong, 1889.

STANLEY, ARTHUR PENRHYN, *The Life and Correspondence of Thomas Arnold, D.D., Late Headmaster of Rugby School, and Regius Professor of Modern History in the University of Oxford*. Boston: Fields, 1870. 8th Amer. ed.

TALBOT, EDITH ARMSTRONG, *Samuel Chapman Armstrong: A Biographical Study*. New York: Doubleday, Page, 1904.

TAYLOR, HOWARD, AND MRS. M. G. G. TAYLOR, *Hudson Taylor and the China Inland Mission: The Growth of a Work of God*. London: Morgan, 1918.

WALKER, F. DEAVILLE, *William Carey, Missionary, Pioneer, and Statesman*. London: Student Christian Movement, 1926.

WESLEY, JOHN, *Journal*. New York: Dutton, 1907. 4 vol. (Everyman's Library.)

WRIGHT, HENRY B., *The Will of God and a Man's Lifework*. New York: Association Press, 1912.

INDEX

307

education, need of a campaign of, in the public schools with reference to the, 118

foreign students, friendly relations among, contribute to solution of the, 115

friendship, personal, as a solvent of the, 114

home life of men of other races, contacts with the, as a solvent of the, 114

inspiring aspects of the, 103

Institute of Pacific Relations, contribution of, to solution of the, 111

Institute of Social and Religious Research, scientific study by, of the, 110 f.

international conferences, the contribution of, to solution of the, 112

International Missionary Council, importance of the, for solution of the, 120

interracial conferences, importance of intimate, to the, 111 f.

interracial federation and the, 105 f.

Jerusalem Meeting, findings of, on the, 120 ff.

missionary program, bearing upon the, of the, 103

missions, importance to Christian, of the, 119 f.

press, importance of enlisting the, toward solution of the, 118

program toward solution of the, 108 ff.

St. Paul, teaching of, on the, 108

segregation and the, 104 f.

Sir Robert Hart on the, 104, 106

S. K. Datta on the, 102

solutions of the, attempted, 104 ff.

South African Institute of Race Relations, contribution of, to solution of the, 118

student migrations, importance of, to the, 115

students in the Southern States of the U. S. A. studying the, 109 f.

study of the, value of serious, 109 ff.

unity of the human race demands solution of the, 103

West by spread of corrupt influences intensifies the, 103

World's Student Christian Federation's foreign-student program as a contribution toward solution of the, 115

Racial consciousness intensified by the World War, 102

Racial patriotism, 16 f.

Racial strife bitterest in rural areas, 54

Rainy, Principal Robert, D.D., 189

Ramabai, Pundita, 165

Rauschenbusch, Walter, 131

Reconciliation, apostles of, 188 ff.

Recruitment, missionary, 224 f., 228, 239 ff.

Red Cross, 222

Reddi, Mrs., vice-president of the Madras Legislative Council, 38

Reform, All-India Women's Conference on Educational and Social, 38

Reforms, Japanese women's agitation for various, 35 f.

Reisner, Dr. John H., 62, 63, 71 ff.

Religious education, see Education

Religious liberty, 187

Religious trends and outlook, 45 ff.

Retreats, 156, 210

Rhodes Trust and similar foundations, 20

Ritson, Dr. J. H., 242

Roberts, George A., 63

Roman Catholic Church, 16, 47

Ross, Professor E. A., 53

Ross, Dr. Emory, 77 f., 98

Round Table Conference, London, 15, 39

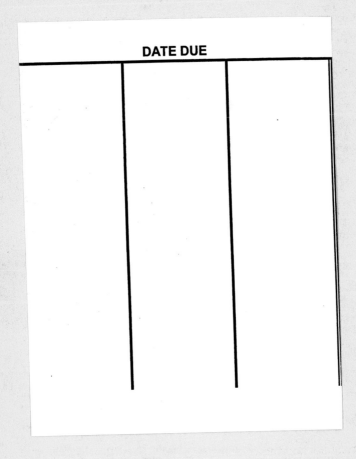

DATE DUE